ACASTOS

ACASTOS

Two Platonic Dialogues

I R I S M U R D O C H

VIKING

To Michael Kustow

VIKING
Viking Penguin Inc.
40 West 23rd Street,
New York, New York 10010, U.S.A.

First American Edition
Published in 1987

LIBRARY OF CONGRESS CATALOGING IN PUBLICATION DATA
Murdoch, Iris.
    Acastos: two Platonic dialogues.
    Contents: Art and Eros — Above the gods.
    1. Socrates—Drama. 2. Plato—Drama. 3. Dialogues,
English. 4. Imaginary conversations.   I. Murdoch, Iris.
Above the gods. 1987.   II. Title.
PR6063.U7A88   1987   822'.914   86-45844
ISBN 0-670-80074-0

Printed in the United States of America by
R. R. Donnelley & Sons Company, Harrisonburg, Virginia
Set in Sabon

CONTENTS

ART AND EROS
A Dialogue about Art

Characters in order of appearance

CALLISTOS   *a beautiful youth*

ACASTOS   *a serious youth*

MANTIAS   *a political man, in love with Callistos*

DEXIMENES   *a cynical man*

PLATO

SOCRATES

Athens in the late fifth century B.C.

At the time of the dialogue, Plato is about twenty years old, Socrates about sixty.

Acastos, Callistos, Mantias and Deximenes are fictional characters.

The first performance of *Art and Eros* took place as a National Theatre Platform Performance in February 1980. The cast was as follows:

SOCRATES   Andrew Cruikshank

PLATO   Greg Hicks

ACASTOS   Adam Norton

CALLISTOS   Robin McDonald

MANTIAS   Anthony Douse

DEXIMENES   Michael Beint

The director was Michael Kustow

At the house of Deximenes.
Enter Callistos, Acastos, Mantias, Deximenes and Plato.
Callistos carries an actor's mask.
Plato sits apart.
They have just come from the theatre.

CALLISTOS
Oh wasn't it great? That last scene was just – *perfect* – Oh I did
enjoy the play! Didn't you, Acastos?

ACASTOS
I'm not sure.

DEXIMENES
Acastos never knows what he feels.

CALLISTOS
You must know what you feel, who else could?

MANTIAS
Is Socrates coming?

CALLISTOS
Oh I do hope Socrates will come!

MANTIAS
Stop jumping around!

CALLISTOS
Did you like the play, Plato?

DEXIMENES
Did you like it?

MANTIAS
No, I never do.

DEXIMENES
Why do you go then?

MANTIAS
One must keep an eye on the theatre, it's an influence.

CALLISTOS
I believe it all when it is happening.

ACASTOS
They say you shouldn't do that, you should sort of realise that
it's a play, and –

MANTIAS
How can you not with actors speaking in those pretentious
unnatural voices!

DEXIMENES
Plays aren't serious. The theatre is cheap magic. Toys for conceited directors. A chance for half-educated people to think
they've understood something. It's unimportant.

MANTIAS
Nothing people like so much is unimportant.

CALLISTOS
Yes, everybody loves the theatre, not just us intellectuals.

Laughter

DEXIMENES
Art is all in the mind. It's not in the play. We invent the art
experience ourselves.

ACASTOS
So we all have different ones?

MANTIAS

I must say I think the theatre's done everything now, after what we've had today. We've seen it all!

DEXIMENES

People always think their art is the end of art.

Callistos, who has been playing with his actor's mask, suddenly puts it on and begins to declaim:

CALLISTOS

Zeus, whoever he may be,
If he cares to bear this name –

MANTIAS

Oh shut up!

DEXIMENES

The theatre is humbug. But who wants it to be like life, it's escape.

CALLISTOS

Yes, who wants it to be like horrid old life? It's a dream world.

DEXIMENES

Monkey business on the stage and private fantasies in the audience!

MANTIAS

It's magic all right. Did you see that audience? How many people? Ten thousand? All sitting absolutely silent and spellbound. Why should they? Why do they *stay* there? Theatre is a kind of miracle, it's an *influence*. Magic can be very useful.

CALLISTOS

You want everything to be useful. Why don't you just enjoy it?

DEXIMENES

He's a politician!

Callistos starts eating some fruit.

MANTIAS
That isn't just for you. Can't you wait? Don't play with it!

CALLISTOS
Oh, you're so socially minded! I think politics should know its place.

MANTIAS
In our society its place is everywhere.

CALLISTOS
Sometimes I think a tyranny would be so relaxing, you wouldn't have to think about politics at all.

ACASTOS
We'll never have tyranny here, after all we *invented* democracy – Yes, I did enjoy the play, and it moved me – but I don't know why.

MANTIAS
Precisely.

ACASTOS
But all sorts of things move us and we don't know why.

MANTIAS
I think we should find out why people are moved.

DEXIMENES
You mean some of us should, so as to control the others!

CALLISTOS
All beauty is like that – it's mysterious –

ACASTOS
Yes – And aren't we forgetting that the plays are a religious festival?

DEXIMENES
Of course we are!

ACASTOS
I don't like seeing the gods portrayed on the stage – after all, how do we know what the gods are like? It's irreverent –

CALLISTOS
You are so old-fashioned. We know what we think about the gods.

ACASTOS
Do we? I don't.

MANTIAS
Religion is important. We shouldn't become too familiar with our gods.

CALLISTOS
There's nothing wrong with irreverence, look at Aristophanes.

DEXIMENES
Well, look at him! [*gesture of disgust*]

MANTIAS
Satire can be influential, it matters what people laugh at.

ACASTOS
I don't think people should laugh at religion, but I think it's good if they can laugh at politicians!

MANTIAS
He who laughs at religion one day will despise his rulers the next. Democracies can perish because in the end people don't believe in anything and don't revere anything.

Enter Socrates. They all rise.

SOCRATES
Well, my dears, did you enjoy the play?

ACASTOS
We were just arguing about it, sir.

CALLISTOS
Bags I sit next to Socrates!

SOCRATES
It's my lucky day!

DEXIMENES
Yes, I saw who you were sitting next to in the theatre.

SOCRATES
I have always worshipped beauty. Who's over there?

CALLISTOS
Plato, he's got one of his moods!

SOCRATES
What was your argument about?

DEXIMENES
Here we go!

CALLISTOS
Deximenes thinks the theatre is magic so it's *not* important, and Mantias thinks the theatre is magic so it *is* important, and Acastos thinks we shouldn't portray the gods, and Mantias thinks it's bad to laugh at people and –

SOCRATES
And what do you think?

CALLISTOS
I think it's fun!

MANTIAS
We were wondering what the theatre was for.

DEXIMENES
Need it be for anything?

CALLISTOS
Everything is for something, isn't it, Socrates?

DEXIMENES
What are you for?

MANTIAS
Need you ask?

SOCRATES
He is young and will have many uses!

ACASTOS
Deximenes says the theatre is false. Can one say that art is true or false?

MANTIAS
I'd rather say good or bad, that is, good or bad for us.

ACASTOS
But you're assuming –

SOCRATES
Wait, wait, not so fast. This is a difficult question. Shall we try to sort it out?

DEXIMENES
You sort it out, Socrates, we'll listen.

SOCRATES
Shall I ask questions and get someone to answer?

DEXIMENES
Who is to stop you, my dear?

SOCRATES
Who shall answer? Let us have the youngest, then if he makes mistakes he need not blush.

DEXIMENES
Who is the youngest?

MANTIAS
Callistos is.

CALLISTOS *alarmed*
No, no, Plato is younger.

SOCRATES
I think Plato is communing with a god and we should not interrupt him. You shall answer.

CALLISTOS
Well, all right, but please don't be cross if –

DEXIMENES
Socrates is never cross.

SOCRATES
Dear child! Perhaps we should start by considering art in general, and then move from the general to the particular. Do you agree?

MANTIAS
Yes, yes, yes.

SOCRATES
We speak, don't we, of 'the arts' as a *family*. But isn't it *odd* that we should classify them together when they are so unlike? It seems that we can see a common quality. Shall we attempt a definition of art?

ACASTOS
Oh yes!

SOCRATES
Then later we can see whether it can be called true or false, or good or bad, or whether it has a use. This won't be easy, I think. Now since you are the victim today, how would you define art?

CALLISTOS
Well, art is the *Odyssey* and the *Agamemnon* and the *Antigone* and the statue of Athena in the Parthenon and music and –

SOCRATES
Wait a moment, this list could go on for ever! These are *examples* of art. But what is the 'artiness' which makes all these different things art?

CALLISTOS
You mean all art, any art?

SOCRATES
Yes.

CALLISTOS
Well – art is copying.

MANTIAS
Why do you suddenly say that?

SOCRATES
What do you mean by copying?

CALLISTOS
I mean like – like paintings – or like imitations of men and animals like you see on the Acropolis. Art tries to be like what things are really like.

SOCRATES
And the best art is the most like?

CALLISTOS
Yes.

MANTIAS
You're contradicting what you said just now —

SOCRATES
So is sculpture a better art than painting?

CALLISTOS
Well — er —

SOCRATES
Painters represent men in two dimensions whereas sculptors represent them in three dimensions.

DEXIMENES
Be brave!

CALLISTOS
Yes, that's better — and the theatre is the best of all because the actors are real men imitating real men.

ACASTOS   *very fast*
That can't be right, if you mean imitation like comparing a statue with a man. Old statues which don't look like real people are often much better art — and if we just want to imitate real things why have art at all? Real men are more like men than marble men are. Or why not just put a cooking pot on a pedestal and call it art, or a few old bricks or — ?

DEXIMENES
If they were called art at least we'd look at them.

MANTIAS
What does music imitate?

SOCRATES
Don't bully him. Perhaps you would like to restate your definition.

CALLISTOS
Yes, well music doesn't seem to copy anything. A play tells a
story of course, and that's like life —

DEXIMENES
Is it?

SOCRATES
Go on, my child, try again.

CALLISTOS
Art is like a sort of form or diagram, it's like life only sort of
different, like summarised or simplified or —

SOCRATES
Do you want to give up your idea that art is copying, imitation
of life?

CALLISTOS
No, but it's copying into a world where everything looks
different and clearer, and there's no muddle and no horrid
accidental things like in life.

ACASTOS
No horrid accidental things!

CALLISTOS
It's like a map.

DEXIMENES
How dull.

SOCRATES
Art is a sort of formal copying into a medium where things look
similar but clearer and simpler?

CALLISTOS
Yes!

MANTIAS
Before you came Callistos was saying art was fabulous and marvellous and beautiful and made him happy and so on! Why don't you say that now? Why did you suddenly say that art is copying?

CALLISTOS *smugly*
Because I know Socrates likes a clear answer even if it's wrong.

SOCRATES
Why did you start by talking about painting?

CALLISTOS
It seems most like what art's really like, I mean here's the thing and here's the picture and you can sort of measure the one against the other.

MANTIAS
Do stop saying 'sort of'!

SOCRATES
Yes, and we often express ideas in visual images, as when we say of music that it's high or low. I'm touched that you tried to please me by saying something clear. But perhaps your idea is still too simple. You spoke of an exact copy, then you spoke of a schematic copy, like a map. Don't you want to add something? When you came out of the theatre you were excited and happy –

MANTIAS
I think we should start again –

Mantias is trying from now on to take over the argument. Acastos also wants to speak and keeps raising his hand. Socrates checks them with a gesture.

CALLISTOS
Yes, when I said about forms and maps that sounds dull, and

art isn't dull, it's emotion and excitement and some art is thrilling like music or when you're in the theatre and you don't know what on earth it's about but your heart *beats* and – of course painting isn't exciting like that –

DEXIMENES
Oh come on – isn't it – sometimes?

CALLISTOS *puzzled for a moment*
You mean like pictures, like those *special* pictures in Derkon's house which show – ? Yes, but that's *sex*.

DEXIMENES
Isn't art about sex?

CALLISTOS
Well –

DEXIMENES
Don't blush, you can't shock Socrates.

SOCRATES
He looks charming.

ACASTOS
Of course we all have kinds of pictures of – But those horrible erotic scenes in Derkon's house aren't art at all, they're just designed to –

DEXIMENES
Acastos is such a puritan, almost as bad as Plato.

ACASTOS
Well, what does Plato think?

He turns to Plato, but Plato ignores him.

MANTIAS
What's the matter with him?

DEXIMENES
Jealousy. He wants Socrates all to himself.

MANTIAS
I see he's taking notes again. Socrates told him not to.

SOCRATES
Go on, hold on to your idea, you've just discovered something you want to add, so perhaps you might now restate your definition.

CALLISTOS
You mean with sex in?

SOCRATES
Anything you like in.

DEXIMENES
You needn't call it sex, call it passion.

SOCRATES
What does music do?

CALLISTOS
It expresses feelings and emotions and makes you feel as if the musical pattern went straight into your heart, into your body.

SOCRATES
Don't you want to put something like that into your definition?

DEXIMENES
Oh come on!

CALLISTOS
Art is the expression of feeling, the communication of emotion. All art is like music really.

SOCRATES
You said it was like painting. Now you say it is like music. You

used the word pattern. *Now* do you want to give up your idea that art imitates the world, in some way?

CALLISTOS
It won't do for music – unless music copies something we can't see or hear.

SOCRATES
Some say that the gods are always doing geometry. Perhaps they are always composing music too.

ACASTOS
I like that – and we sometimes overhear a little.

CALLISTOS
But art *is* about the world, how real things are changed into a sort of feeling-pattern, a feeling-thought or – sorry, I'm in a muddle –

SOCRATES
Go on, dear boy, don't give up, try to catch something here. Remember, you are doing philosophy – and sometimes when you've been trying really hard to get a glimpse of an idea you can only talk about it in a kind of nonsense. So stop trying to be clear and just talk honest nonsense.

CALLISTOS *trying hard*
Art is a sort of copying or imitating, because it *is* about the real world somehow, though I'm not sure about music, and it has a pattern and form, so it does change things, it's sort of neater and clearer than life, but it shows us real things with great – *force* – with *emotion* – and through seeing and hearing and imagining – and it's not sort of *analysed*, it's all condensed into one, like a *thing* – and it's exciting and sexy and – oh dear –

SOCRATES
No, no, you've done very well. You've talked most excellent

nonsense and helped our argument along splendidly. You said art was like a realistic picture, then you said it was like a map, then you said it was like music where an emotional pattern enters into the body. And just now you spoke of seeing and hearing and imagining. Are all arts something to do with the senses?

CALLISTOS
Yes, I think so –

ACASTOS
But –

SOCRATES
Acastos has been waving his hand at me for some time, let us hear what he has to say.

ACASTOS
I agree that art is to do with the senses – I mean poetry has rhythms and sounds and pictures have shapes and colours, and the body is involved, I don't mean like sex –

DEXIMENES
Why not?

ACASTOS
But really art is *thinking*. I mean, good art is deep wise thinking. And bad art is bad because it's stupid or depraved thinking. Callistos said something about a 'feeling-thought'. I don't know what that is. But I'm sure good art *tells* us something. It isn't just a dose of emotion. It's like vision – insight – knowledge –

SOCRATES
Good, good, you are continuing Callistos's splendid nonsense! Copying, maps, feeling, thinking. Yes, we use all these ideas to help each other out, as each one by itself seems helpless. But

still the ideas remain obscure, they stand as it were in a ring holding hands and each idea tries to support the next but cannot support itself. Do you want to keep Callistos's idea that art is imitation of the world?

ACASTOS
Yes, but not simple like a real man and a marble man, it's *indirect*.

CALLISTOS
I said it was different!

ACASTOS
The artist puts thoughts in, he's a judge of reality.

SOCRATES
A judge suggests justice – truth –

ACASTOS
Yes, the idea of copying and judging means *truth* and *morality*. Art has got to be *true*. Deximenes said art is trickery and fantasy and perhaps bad art is, but good art is wisdom and truth. Art is looking at the world and explaining it in a *deep* way and when we understand the explanation or even half understand it we feel oh – such joy – and I think that's what *beauty* is –

DEXIMENES
What about beauty in nature? Nature doesn't explain!

Callistos, let off the hook, pats himself on the back, plays with the mask, tries to put it onto Mantias, who thrusts him away. Plato is listening attentively to what Acastos is saying.

ACASTOS
A man could copy cleverly, like in pornographic pictures, but if there's no moral judgement and no thought the thing is dead

and false. Callistos said art was sexy and I suppose it is
sometimes, but I'd rather say it was to do with love, with really
loving the world and seeing what it's like. I think good art is
passionate and holy.

SOCRATES
I like that, I like that –

ACASTOS
And it's *somehow* true – I'm certain of that –

SOCRATES
Hold on to that certainty, my dear young friend.

*Slight pause. Socrates glances at Plato, but Plato will not be
drawn in. He drops his head sulkily.*

I like your instincts. The good artist is wise, compassionate,
just – but we're in deep waters. You'll have to think more
carefully about what you mean by saying that good art is true.

DEXIMENES
Poetry isn't *true*! This is getting too awfully high-minded for
me.

ACASTOS   *increasingly excited by his ideas but confused*
I mean, I think good art is *good* for us, it *teaches* us – great
poetry is *wise* –

CALLISTOS   *he has donned the mask again and begins to
declaim*
Zeus, whoever he may be,
If he cares to bear this name –

MANTIAS
All this woolly talk has simply brought us to the obvious point
which I wanted to make at the start! At last Acastos has quite
accidentally said something sensible! He says good art is good

for us! That's the whole thing in a nutshell. It's educational.
Socrates said your ideas were standing in a circle holding hands
and each trying to explain the next and couldn't. My idea
breaks the circle. If we think of art as education everything
becomes clear, it answers all the questions – it's clear why we
classify the arts together, it makes sense of music, it clarifies this
notion of morality which Acastos has introduced –

ACASTOS
I don't mean that art is education.

MANTIAS
You said so!

ACASTOS
I said it was good for us.

MANTIAS
What's the difference? I'm concerned with politics and social
life, unlike some who are only interested in their own little
messy private feelings. Politics is not self centred, it's to do with
other people, with caring, with society. The essence of politics
is explanation, that is persuasive explanation.

DEXIMENES
I thought the essence of politics was coercion.

MANTIAS
I said *persuasive* explanation, another name for this is rhetoric.
And this explains the nature of art. Art is rhetoric. Not copying
or music or thought. Rhetoric.

SOCRATES
You stun us with the simplicity of your idea.

MANTIAS
Well it's so clear. And that's how we distinguish between good

and bad art. Good art makes good citizens, bad art makes bad citizens. It's as simple as that.

SOCRATES
Do you *define* good art as art which benefits society?

MANTIAS   *after hesitation but firmly*
Yes.

ACASTOS
Oh no!

CALLISTOS
Horrid!

MANTIAS
The really useful and valuable arts are the ones which make plain statements, stuff you can understand.

DEXIMENES
Lots of poetry is very obscure, or personal, or erotic.

MANTIAS
Art which is private and obsessive is bad, it distracts people from the real world, the *public* world. I should have thought that's obvious and should be of interest to Acastos with his concern for truth! And erotic art makes people think that sex is the whole point of life!

CALLISTOS
Isn't it?

DEXIMENES
All art can be used as pornography. Art happens in the mind. Even great art isn't sacred. We all have obsessions.

MANTIAS
You have.

CALLISTOS
Sex is *funny*!

MANTIAS
An art which is solely concerned with sex and personal relations is selfish and untruthful. Wouldn't you agree, Acastos?

Acastos is not sure.

SOCRATES
Isn't it the nature of art to explore the relation between the
public and the private? Art turns us inside out, it exhibits what
is secret. What goes on inwardly in the soul is the essence of
each man, it's what makes us individual people. The relation
between that inwardness and public conduct *is morality.* How
can art ignore it?

DEXIMENES
Mantias doesn't believe in individual people.

MANTIAS
Yes, I do! That's just what I do believe in and you don't! Art
must overcome the *alienation* of men from each other. It
should try to make *sense* of society. [*To Acastos*] That's better
than private fantasy, isn't it?

DEXIMENES
If you ban private personal relations you ban the whole of art.

MANTIAS
Our painting and our sculpture represent people who are
physically healthy. I think our arts should represent people
who are morally healthy!

SOCRATES
Who are these people?

MANTIAS

Good citizens.

DEXIMENES

I know, healthy handsome young men performing valuable social duties!

MANTIAS

All right, you jeer at the idea of the good citizen! What have *you* ever done with all that cleverness and idealism you had when we were *their* age?

Deximenes is hurt.

I'm sorry. This society is full of injustice and misery. Isn't it, Acastos? Yes or no?

ACASTOS

Yes.

MANTIAS

Won't the whole man, the decent man, try to change this, won't he devote all he has to changing it? Why should artists be exempt? Why shouldn't they use their talents to help their society? Art is a thought concealed in an emotional package, as Acastos said –

ACASTOS

I didn't – I don't think I did –

MANTIAS

Emotion is important but it must be simplified –

SOCRATES

Callistos made a distinction between realistic copying, and formal schematic representation, like a map. What would your simplified art be like?

MANTIAS
Formal and schematic, but realistic enough to be plausible. The
meaning must be clear to everybody.

DEXIMENES
And not just to us intellectuals, as Callistos would say!

MANTIAS
Precisely. Intellectuals are usually self-indulgent people who
think refined private thoughts and neglect the public good.

ACASTOS
But you're an intellectual!

DEXIMENES
He's a boss-type intellectual.

ACASTOS
You want art to be propaganda!

MANTIAS
Art is education. All education propagates values. They may as
well be the right values. No?

ACASTOS
But if it's propaganda and persuasion it isn't true!

MANTIAS
Socrates told you to think what you mean by 'true'. When we
make moral judgements on people we're trying to persuade
them, we're trying to affect their conduct, aren't we – *aren't
we?*

ACASTOS
Well –

MANTIAS
You admire Pericles, don't you?

ACASTOS
Yes.

MANTIAS
Wasn't he a persuader, a great rhetorician, all those marvellous speeches? – You've got to *encourage* your citizens, make them confident, proud of their state –

DEXIMENES
Give them a glorious past!

MANTIAS
It matters how we see our past, that's obvious.

DEXIMENES
Some things are better forgotten, some things must never be forgotten!

ACASTOS
We never let anyone forget that we defeated the Persians!

MANTIAS
All right! Every country has a selective tradition. Most Persians have probably never heard of the Battle of Marathon!

ACASTOS
What you call selective tradition is lying! We ought to tell the truth about the past.

MANTIAS
You keep on using the word 'truth' as if it were some sort of decisive weapon, or even a reasonably clear idea. History is persuasive speculation, it's fabulation. What can we know about 'what really happened'? Literature *invents* the past, that's why it's so important, it must go on inventing the past that the present needs!

ACASTOS
You make it all sound like lying!

MANTIAS
It's bound to be what you call lying, I want it to be useful purified lying.

DEXIMENES
'Purified lying' – that's good!

MANTIAS
Art isn't like nature, even 'realism' isn't, words can't express things, they can't go out and touch them, words aren't names –

SOCRATES
Wait a moment. You say we can't know the past, we can only make up useful stories about it. Now you're talking about language generally. You mean words can't picture reality at all?

MANTIAS
That's what I mean!

SOCRATES
How do you know? Do you look at words and then at reality and –

MANTIAS *floundering*
I mean – really there's no such thing as 'reality' or 'nature', it's not just sitting there, we *make* it out of words – ideas – concepts –

ACASTOS
So language doesn't refer to the world?

SOCRATES
Wait, we must see what Mantias is up to, what he really *wants*, metaphysicians usually *want* something or other. Of course

words are not just names, the operation of language is very complicated, we use all sorts of conceptual tricks to relate to our surroundings, we often disagree about how to do it. It certainly does *not* follow from this that there is no independent world such as common sense takes for granted.

DEXIMENES *knocking a table*
Of course there's an independent world.

SOCRATES
Not a bad argument!

MANTIAS
It's a stupid argument, as you perfectly well know. Language has meaning through internal coherence, it's not like a window we look through.

SOCRATES
Well, sometimes it's like a window, and often it's not coherent. Perhaps you are thinking of mathematics or of some language used by the gods. Our natural mortal language is a much more messy business and very difficult to theorise about. Let us say that your hypothesis is interesting but rather far-fetched! Our language is being broken and tested and altered all the time in relation to *something else* which certainly *seems* to be 'just sitting there', quite pleased with itself, and indifferent to our ingenuity and our wishes! This is our most evident and primary experience. Of course it is mysterious, consciousness itself is the most mysterious thing of all, and philosophers feel challenged by mysteries. But philosophy can't always say something systematic and universal and marvellous! Faced with something so very – difficult – I think we should be careful and modest and hold on to common sense and our ordinary conceptions of truth. Reality resists us, it is contingent, it transcends us, it surprises us, language is a *struggle*, we live on a borderline –

ACASTOS *bursting in*
We must have words *and* reality or we can't distinguish true
and false!

SOCRATES
I think Mantias would like to blur or reinterpret that distinction, that is his point, that is what his metaphysical theory is
for. He would like to substitute useful or useless, or coherent or
noncoherent, or perhaps significant-now and not significant-
now. He would regard this as a *political* idea of some importance.

MANTIAS
Yes, and an obvious one too! Language makes men, it *speaks*
men, it determines what they see and understand – it's not just
an adventure playground for writers – it must be made to *work*
in the present and *serve* society –

SOCRATES
So really language is not description, it's more like orders?

MANTIAS
Well, yes – I mean, we don't want to explain the world, we
want to change it!

ACASTOS
But if words aren't true or false what are *we* doing now arguing
with each other?

DEXIMENES
We are exempt, Acastos! People who talk like Mantias always
exclude themselves from their generalisations! It's only the
simple folk who talk like parrots!

MANTIAS
All right, but let's not be too modest, very few people can
invent concepts and ideas –

DEXIMENES

That's the new tyranny in a nutshell, a programme for tyrants!
A few rulers manipulating the language, and the mass of
ordinary chaps enjoying plausible simple social art! Words
perish, and nobody can speak the truth!

ACASTOS *fast*

Socrates says we live on a borderline, yes, we're *all* out there,
using words and inventing concepts and struggling with reality
and keeping the language alive and making it say true things,
and that's why literature is so important, and –

CALLISTOS

Jokes are works of art too!

SOCRATES

Yes, good! [*Everyone is trying to talk*.] Be quiet, my children! I
don't want this argument to become too abstract and lose its
bite. In philosophy you must locate your problem [*gestures*]
and then hold it firmly and turn it round to see its different
faces. Now – Acastos sees art as essentially free reflection and
truth-telling, Mantias sees it as carefully planted signposts to
good and bad, or rather useful and useless –

MANTIAS

Yes, that's what I mean by good and bad. Writers should take
sides with good. [*To Acastos*] You can't disagree with that!

ACASTOS

If you detach writers from ordinary free truth they'll just play
with language!

MANTIAS

They should portray good men in a clear intelligent way, and
show them overcoming bad men.

SOCRATES
So they will portray bad men too?

MANTIAS
Yes, but the bad men must not be interesting or attractive, they
must be schematically represented —

ACASTOS
You mean caricatured?

MANTIAS
And never shown as successful.

SOCRATES
Yet in real life bad men are often both interesting and successful. And good men are often dull, because they are quiet and
steady, whereas bad men are unstable and odd.

ACASTOS
Surely there are plenty of interesting good men in literature.

SOCRATES
Name some.

DEXIMENES
Who are our great literary heroes? Crooks to a man. Achilles,
the biggest egoist ever. Odysseus, a swindler and a liar. The
whole cast of the stupid pointless Trojan war are one lot of
ruthless thugs against another lot.

ACASTOS
Hector.

DEXIMENES
Proves my point, a nonentity. Who doesn't side with Achilles?

ACASTOS
I don't.

CALLISTOS
My dear, Achilles is a Greek!

DEXIMENES
Agamemnon, a power-crazy general, Clytemnestra, a murderer, Antigone, a selfish opinionated trouble-maker. And some of the greatest crooks of all are the gods. No wonder no one believes in them any more.

ACASTOS
I believe in the gods.

CALLISTOS
So does Socrates.

DEXIMENES
No, the religious era is over. Who's going to believe those stories now? Who really thinks that Zeus is an old man with a beard somewhere up there?

CALLISTOS *softly*
Zeus, whoever he may be —

ACASTOS
Some people say the myths are true but sort of symbolic. What do you think, Socrates?

SOCRATES
I think that religion will always be with us, and we shall continually remake it into something we can believe. You see, we want to be certain that goodness rests upon reality. And as this desire will never go away, we shall always be searching for the gods. We want to love what is pure and holy, and to know that it is *safe*.

ACASTOS
Safe?

SOCRATES
Inviolable, indestructible, *real.*

CALLISTOS
But do the gods exist?

SOCRATES
Here we reach the end of what words can do. The gods concern the inmost heart of each man – and about this he can only speak to himself – and to them.

ACASTOS
Can't we always invent language, like poets do?

SOCRATES
There is a very great distance between the human and the divine. We must hope the gods will come to us. Perhaps there is something in us which belongs to them and which they will claim – in their own way. A man should follow virtue and look toward the good – and be content to *know* what he cannot *say.*

ACASTOS
But – *does* goodness rest upon reality?

SOCRATES   *just for Acastos*
Yes, my dear.

MANTIAS
No sensible politician wants to destroy religion. Religion is an image of authority. People must take the exercise of authority for granted. That is the mystery of government, that men will obey other men, and that many men will obey few men. Nothing could be more disastrous for a state than the disappearance of a generally accepted religion. As soon as the myth of government is challenged the state descends into anarchy.

ACASTOS
You call it a myth.

MANTIAS
It's the most important myth of all. *Obedience.*

ACASTOS
You talk as if ordinary people were stupid or semi-criminal.

MANTIAS
Any practical politician assumes that! Of course the state must control art. If it doesn't it is wasting a precious source of power. All that emotion in the theatre today, wasted, just rising up uselessly into the sky! What an energy loss!

SOCRATES
What is such control usually called?

MANTIAS
Censorship.

ACASTOS
I'm against it.

CALLISTOS
Me too.

SOCRATES
We must not be afraid of names.

MANTIAS
Every state exercises some censorship. [*To Acastos*] Do you want pornographic muck to circulate, like those pictures you hate so? Would you like children to see them?

ACASTOS
Well – no – but –

MANTIAS
And you're so keen on the rights of minorities, under-privileged groups or whatever jargon you use. Would you like

to see plays in our theatres which encourage people to be unkind to slaves and women?

DEXIMENES
They don't need encouragement.

MANTIAS
You say slavery is contrary to nature. Don't you want to silence
people who say slaves are just animals?

DEXIMENES
Acastos thinks animals have rights too!

MANTIAS
Well things then.

DEXIMENES
Things lib!

MANTIAS
Art must not stir up useless violence or make us hate people just
because they're foreigners –

CALLISTOS
Can't we hate anyone, not even bloody Spartans?

DEXIMENES
Arguments like this are futile because they assume that we can
change things – we can't. None of us can control the state, even
tyrants can't. We always talk as if *we* could, we, the intellectuals. But no one controls it – it's a machine that rolls on
under its own laws. Who understands economics? The econo-
mists don't, how can we? We are passengers not drivers in this
chariot. There are no drivers.

MANTIAS
People say that who haven't the wit to see who the drivers are!
That sort of talk leads straight to tyranny or mob rule!

DEXIMENES
What about you? – You'd be arresting poets because you couldn't understand their poems!

ACASTOS
I suppose your dull bad art could do some good –

DEXIMENES
Like stories telling children to wash!

MANTIAS
Then you agree with me!

ACASTOS
No! I don't want to argue your argument at all – I mean – Oh help me, Socrates!

SOCRATES
Well, we could discuss whether censorship or freedom is better – but I think Acastos wants to say that we have lost sight of our original objective. If we could discover what art really is we would also see how it relates to society.

CALLISTOS
Oh let's forget society!

SOCRATES
Now you wish to *define* art in terms of its social role, and this is what Acastos objects to. [*Acastos is nodding agreement*] Now would you agree that art is a skill?

MANTIAS
Yes.

SOCRATES
And properly to understand a skill one must understand what it is to exercise it well? Very well?

MANTIAS *dubiously*
Yes.

ACASTOS
That's it, Mantias won't really *look* at what I call good art.

SOCRATES
You have different views of what the skill *is*. So you must reject his definition.

ACASTOS
I do, I refuse to define good art as good-for-society art. Art must be free and on its own because that's how it will tell us the truth and show us the things that are really – high – and real – I mean, it's like the human spirit talking – good art just can't help being good for society, but artists mustn't think about that. Good artists are trying to understand something and show something which they see – their duty is to be good artists. Good art explains to us how the world is changing and it judges change, it's the highest wisest voice of morality, it's something spiritual – without good art a society dies. It's like religion really – it's our best speech and our best understanding – it's a proof of the greatness and goodness which is in us and –

DEXIMENES
And everything follows from that, I suppose, including the liberation of slaves and women!

ACASTOS
Yes!

SOCRATES
What a Protean monster our art turns out to be! Copies, maps, thoughts, music, games, rhetoric, social service, and now religion!

CALLISTOS
My head's spinning. Pass the wine, old cock.

DEXIMENES
Old cock!

ACASTOS
You see – what we call inspiration –

DEXIMENES
He's off again.

Plato utters a low groan.

SOCRATES
Did I hear a sound? Did young Plato utter an observation? Or
did some passing god groan over our follies?

PLATO
Oh what nonsense you all talk! I don't mean Socrates but he's
just making you hold forth and not correcting you.

DEXIMENES
You correct us then, *dear* boy!

SOCRATES
We have so far lacked the benefit of your opinion.

PLATO
Oh it's so –

CALLISTOS
Plato's so emotional and extreme, he gets so cross!

DEXIMENES
You mean he takes it all seriously.

CALLISTOS
There's no need to be rude.

SOCRATES
Would you like to join our conversation?

PLATO
Yes.

DEXIMENES
Yes, please.

SOCRATES
Then be a little kind to us. If you roar at us like a wild beast we shall be too frightened to talk to you.

DEXIMENES
I'd box his ears for him.

CALLISTOS
Of course we are philosophers and Plato is a poet so we must make allowances –

ACASTOS
At least you can tell us who you agree with.

PLATO
I agree with Deximenes.

Laughter.

CALLISTOS
You can't!

DEXIMENES
I'm touched by this unexpected tribute.

PLATO
Art is lies, it's fantasy, it's play, it's humbug, it's make-believe, the theatre is rubbish, it's –

SOCRATES
Dear boy, don't shout at us. Either talk seriously and honestly
or go away.

PLATO
And I think philosophy is lies too.

ACASTOS
How can you say that in front of Socrates!

PLATO
I'm sorry –

SOCRATES
That can be argued also, by a philosophical argument. If you
want to talk to us you must join this discussion, not start
another one. You have been listening to us and even thought
some of our nonsense worth writing down. But please don't say
what you don't mean.

PLATO
I'm very sorry, but really, you're all so unserious about art, as if
it were a sort of side issue. As if one could say there's the navy
and the silver mines and the war and the latest news about
Alcibiades and this and that and then of course there's art and –
But art is – in a way it's almost *everything* – you don't see how
deep art is, and how *awful* it is!

CALLISTOS
I think your poems are rather nice.

SOCRATES
Explain yourself, my dear Plato, since you've found your
tongue at last, and do it *quietly*.

PLATO
Art is full of horrible things which it makes us accept –

DEXIMENES

Life is full of horrible things, why shouldn't art be?

PLATO

Life is accidental, art isn't. You were talking about Achilles and how we all love him and we *identify* with him. But he slaughters all those Trojan prisoners beside the funeral pyre of Patroclus. And Odysseus, whom everyone admires, when he comes home he hangs all the servant girls just because they went to bed with the suitors. And he murders all the suitors, and this ghastly blood bath is supposed to be great art –

DEXIMENES

Why shouldn't he kill the suitors?

PLATO

There you are! Because it's art you stop thinking! Because it's art you can murder prisoners and hang silly helpless women and slaughter a lot of people who haven't done any harm except hang around your house and propose honourable marriage to your widow, they didn't rape her!

DEXIMENES

But such things happen in life –

PLATO

Yes, but why celebrate them in art? And I agree with Mantias about malicious laughter being evil. So why does Homer show us the gods laughing spitefully at Hephaistos? And this is the poet whom we're all supposed to admire and love.

DEXIMENES

You admire and love him.

PLATO

Yes, but I'm irrational [*laughter*]. And we're all waiting for

Agamemnon to be murdered, we're licking our lips at the idea of Clytemnestra using an axe on her husband –

ACASTOS
You said you agree with Deximenes –

PLATO
Yes, art is erotic, all art is erotic.

CALLISTOS
He means all good art.

DEXIMENES
No, he means all bad art.

PLATO
Even Sophocles –

SOCRATES
Wait, wait, wait, don't just deluge us with examples. You have asked some interesting questions, but let us go along slowly as we have to do in philosophy and not just rush away after every new thing. Let us review our argument so far, and then Plato can leap off the end of it and spread his wings in the air. Callistos said that art was copying, then he said that it was like a map, then he said that it stirred up the emotions and was like music. And Acastos said that it was thinking and truthful vision. And Mantias said that it was rhetoric or propaganda. And Acastos was so shocked by this that he said it was religion.

DEXIMENES
And don't forget my view, which Plato says he agrees with, that art is fantasy. Art objects are fake objects, we invent them ourselves, it's just private fantasy in our minds. Callistos said that art aspires to the condition of music, Acastos said it aspires to the condition of religion, I say it aspires to the condition of pornography.

SOCRATES
Before we proceed I am going to be a little unkind to somebody.

CALLISTOS
Oh not to me!

SOCRATES
No, to Mantias.

MANTIAS
Oh!

SOCRATES
I am going to ask you to put aside your definition of art as a socially useful craft.

MANTIAS
Why?

SOCRATES
Just now I distinguished your question of the *use* of art and Acastos's question about what art is.

MANTIAS
But I define art by its use.

SOCRATES
Many things are socially useful. You say art is a socially useful craft — and if we ask what *sort* of socially useful craft, the answer is, an *artistic* one. But to understand this we must first have a more fundamental idea of what art really is.

MANTIAS
I don't follow —

SOCRATES
Much of what you said about the *effect* of art is important. But we cannot define art by its effect without *first* considering its nature, since other things could produce the same effect.

MANTIAS
Oh all right –

Callistos embraces him.

SOCRATES
Now, my dear splendid clever boy, try to put your thoughts in order, don't just pour them over us like a bath attendant. Think, my child, think, you *can* think.

PLATO   *after holding his head for a moment*
Of course we must ask about good and bad art in order to see what art is. Bad art is nothing, it's fantasy, like we have when we imagine ourselves great and wonderful – or like sentimental rubbish or Mantias's dull improving stories. And of course bad art can be harmful like pornographic muck or like stories designed to make people hate each other – you know – But to see how dangerous and terrible art is we have to see what *good* art is like, why we tolerate it, why we *love* it, why we sit in the theatre –

ACASTOS
What about inspiration?

PLATO
All right, good art is not just selfish fantasy and that's why you want to call it 'true'. But what is this inspiration and how does it differ from what makes us have stupid fantasies and day-dreams? It's something so *deep* –

DEXIMENES
You mean it's erotic.

PLATO
I don't want to use that word, sometimes words are spoilt. I mean something which can be either bad or good –

SOCRATES
Sometimes when words fail us we have to turn to the gods and utter their holy and untainted names.

PLATO
Yes. Let us call it Eros. Art comes from the deep soul where a great force lives, and this force is sex and love and desire – desire for power, desire for possession, sexual desire, desire for beauty, desire for knowledge, desire for God – what makes us good, or bad – and without this force there is no art, and no science either, and no – no man – without Eros man is a ghost. But with Eros he can be – either a demon or – Socrates.

DEXIMENES
Socrates is a good demon.

CALLISTOS
But you do mean sex, don't you?

PLATO
Not in your sense.

ACASTOS
Love, then.

PLATO
Love, what's that? A tyrant loves power, a lecher loves women, Deximenes loves music, or it can be intellectual –

SOCRATES
Theaetetus loves mathematics.

ACASTOS
You mean art comes out of a passion which can be either good or bad, and good art comes out of a good passion, but that's just what I was saying, why it tells truth, and why it must be *free*, and why it does serve society, but not in Mantias's way.

Because of this passion, which is a kind of *vision*, artists can see truth and tell truth, they can tell more truth than anyone else, they can *communicate* it –

PLATO
So you think, I would like to agree, but art is more terrible, more ambiguous, no wonder rulers fear it and want to tame it, as Mantias does, and make it little and mean and small. Art's so attractive, poetry transforms horror and wickedness into beauty. Art can make terrible things into wonderful things and that's the biggest lie of all.

DEXIMENES
Call it a half truth. Can human beings bear more than half the truth? They're lucky to have half. That's what's called escape and thank God for it!

PLATO
Escape! But we must not escape. Art is the highest escape route, it's the last exit, and that is why it is the most dangerous.

DEXIMENES
Since few people ever get as far as your last exit I don't think it matters very much.

CALLISTOS
But what are we escaping *from*?

PLATO
Art is dangerous to philosophy, it's dangerous to religion. It masquerades as the whole truth and makes us content with something less. And people idolise it so, Deximenes said the theatre makes fools think they've understood something. The language of art can also make people who are not fools think they have understood something, it can make them stop going on.

CALLISTOS
Going on *where?*

PLATO
I think – I think that the human mind, the human soul is a vast
region most of which is dark. There are different parts, different levels. There are dark low levels where we are hardly
individual people at all –

*Plato has come nearer to Socrates and speaks to him
eloquently, almost like a lover. Socrates smiles.*

ACASTOS *intently listening*
Is *that* Eros?

PLATO
Eros is there. This darkness is sex, power, desire, inspiration,
energy for good or evil. Many people live their whole lives in
that sort of darkness, seeing nothing but flickering shadows
and illusions, like images thrown on a screen – and the only
energy they ever have comes from egoism and dreams. They
don't know what the real world is like at all. Not only could
they not understand any difficult thought, they cannot even *see*
ordinary things – like that wine cup or the face of Socrates –
because anxiety and selfishness are making them blind, they
live behind a dark veil.

ACASTOS
Do you mean evil people?

DEXIMENES
Sounds like most of us!

PLATO
Then there's another level where people understand a little
about the world and live by habits and a few simple ideas.

CALLISTOS
Dull people.

PLATO
They have illusions too, like accepting conventions and preju-
dices without thinking about them, and being selfish in an
orderly prudent sort of way, buying things for their houses and
so on –

DEXIMENES
That sounds like most of us too!

PLATO
All these people are like – like living in a cave. They see only
shadows, they don't see the real world or the light of the sun.
But then sometimes some people can get out of the cave –

CALLISTOS
This all sounds rather elitist to me.

PLATO
When they get out they're *amazed*, they see real things in the
sunlight, their minds are awakened and they understand – and
oh – the world, when you understand it and can see it, even a
little – can be so beautiful – and the anxiety and the mean
egoism go away and your eyes are unveiled – perhaps it's only
for a short time, because the light of the sun dazzles you – and
you begin to know about what Acastos calls the truth, and see
the difference between truth and falsehood in the clear light of
truth itself –

ACASTOS
Like when you really understand mathematics.

PLATO
Yes, like when you *really* understand anything – And that's
difficult – I don't just mean slick cleverness, I mean something

which shakes the whole soul and opens it out into some huge
brightness and this is love too, when we love real things and see
them distinctly in a clear light.

MANTIAS
What about the people they've left behind in the dark?

PLATO
And when we begin to know and to find out, it's wonderful, it's
like remembering, as if we were coming home to a spiritual
world where we really belong.

MANTIAS
Is this some sort of *religious* theory?

PLATO
And then the highest thing of all, there's wisdom, and all the
things you understand, the hard things, come together somehow, and you see that they're *connected*, and that's real
wisdom, which is goodness and virtue and freedom – real
freedom like what most people who talk about freedom can't
conceive of – and this isn't just intellectual understanding, it's
spiritual, it's what we really think in our hearts about the gods,
like Socrates said – and that's Eros too, the high, the heavenly
Eros, love made perfect and wise and good – and that far far
point, that's truth, seeing everything in the light of the sun –
and then – seeing the sun itself – and that's goodness – and
joy –

DEXIMENES
Dear me.

CALLISTOS
It's those mystery religions, they take drugs, you know.

ACASTOS
This is a bit like something Socrates said once, but you make it

all sound different. Socrates never said that everything was connected.

DEXIMENES
May I ask, are we all living at these different levels all the time?

PLATO
I'm not sure —

ACASTOS
I like your picture — very much — though I can't understand it.

DEXIMENES
Neither can he.

ACASTOS
But where does art come in? Of course I see that a lot of art is just shadows and illusions, images on a flickering screen —

DEXIMENES
The fantasy of the artist arousing the fantasy of the viewer.

ACASTOS
But what about good art?

PLATO
Is there any?

DEXIMENES
Oh come — !

ACASTOS
Yes, of course!

PLATO
Don't we deceive ourselves? We want to worship artists because they save us trouble. They give the illusion of thinking great thoughts. But art is never far from fantasy, and the people who enjoy it degrade it even further! Art isn't something up in

heaven in an airtight box looked after by Apollo, it's just words or pictures which people find attractive!

ACASTOS *confused*
But language does refer to a separate reality, and –

PLATO
That reality is *separate* is my point! Any language depends on some sense of true and false, but language is as good as its user. Most people only believe in themselves, they don't *really* think other people exist, they don't *explore* the real world, it's too difficult and painful, and their language is weak and limited, just a network of illusions. And of course many *high* things can be hard to express, hard to say at all except to somebody else who understands. Language travels with the soul, it becomes purer through trying to tell truth. Reality is difficult to get to, we have to try –

DEXIMENES
You mean we ought to try. But can't we separate truth and goodness?

PLATO
No. They're interlocked. That's just where art misleads us, it seems to remove the difficulty, it produces such a strong impression that we imagine we've arrived, that we're in the presence of something real! Good art can be a kind of image or *imitation* of goodness. That's how it deceives enlightened people and stops them from trying to become better. It's a kind of sacrilege. If you believe in the gods, whatever they may be, you know that they make some absolute pure demand – the highest thing of all – it's like when an athlete in the Games is strained almost beyond endurance, almost to dying. Art softens the demand of the gods. It puts an attractive veil over that *final* awful demand, that final transformation into goodness, the

almost impossible *last step* which is what human life is really all about.

Pause.

DEXIMENES
That's what you meant by the last exit.

MANTIAS
I'm all for religion but this is crazy.

CALLISTOS
I think Plato hates art because he's envious. He's envious of the great poets, he wishes he was one.

PLATO
Art is the final cunning of the human soul which would rather do anything than face the gods.

Pause. Then Socrates chuckles. Plato, who has been exalted, now smiles, spreads his arms, falls on one knee before Socrates.

SOCRATES
You have spoken beautifully and given praise to that and to those to whom praise is due and perhaps with this hymn of praise we ought to end our discussion.

ACASTOS
Oh, no!

SOCRATES
I'm afraid that the simple and homely things which any of us might now wish to say would seem an anti-climax after this paean of eloquence. But since art has found such a potent enemy, perhaps a humble devotee might just say one or two brief things in her defence. We must not be too stunned by our young friend's rhetoric – for he is a persuasive fellow – and he

does what persuaders often do, he makes different things seem
the same, he says good art is 'really' the same as bad art.
Whereas Acastos thinks the difference between them is very
great and important. When we find a generally held distinction
we are wise not to blur it before we look to see if it shows
something true. It may be that the only art you would praise is
practised in heaven when Apollo and the Muses delight the ears
of the other gods. But here below the difference between good
and bad art as we know it remains significant. It is true that we
do often prefer illusions and magic to the hard task of thinking
– and that the *half-truth* may be the comforting place where
we stop trying.

CALLISTOS
I don't see why we should try at all.

SOCRATES   *stroking Callistos's hair*
Callistos asks a good question.

PLATO
We try because our home is elsewhere and it draws us like a
magnet.

SOCRATES
This too is a poetic image and may be a comforting one. You
yourself said earlier that art is everywhere. Callistos unkindly
suggested that you envy the great poets, perhaps you do. Art is a
fundamental method of explanation, and this is what Acastos
was trying to say to us when he talked so well earlier on. And it
is a *natural* mode of explanation for human beings and one
which, in your eloquence, you use yourself. Our home may be
elsewhere, but we are condemned to exile, to live here with our
fellow exiles. And we have to live with language and with
words. You have spoken reverently about what is highest, and
whatever belief we hold about the gods we may understand

you. You say art consoles us and prevents us from taking the final step. You say art is a last exit or a second best. It may be that human beings can only achieve a second best, that second best is our best. [*Plato is shaking his head.*] Perhaps not only art but all our highest speculations, the highest achievements of our spirit are second best. Homer is imperfect. Science is imperfect. Any high thinking of which we are capable is faulty. Not everything connects, my dear Plato. We are not gods. What you call the whole truth is only for them. So our truth must include, must *embrace* the idea of the second best, that all our thought will be incomplete and all our art tainted by selfishness. This doesn't mean there is no difference between the good and the bad in what we achieve. And it doesn't mean not trying. It means trying in a humble modest truthful spirit. *This* is our truth.

PLATO
You mean we can't get all the way.

SOCRATES
No.

PLATO
Philosophy can get all the way.

SOCRATES
No.

PLATO
If I thought that I could not imagine wanting to be a philosopher at all.

DEXIMENES
You will never be a philosopher, you are far too emotional.

SOCRATES

It may even be that, as Acastos says, good art tells us more truth about our lives and our world than any other kind of thinking or speculation – it certainly speaks to more people. And perhaps the language of art is the most universal and *enduring* kind of human thought. We are mixed beings, as you said yourself, mixed of darkness and light, sense and intellect, flesh and spirit – the language of art is the highest native natural language of that condition. And you were right to say that art is not just a rare skill. We are all artists, we are all story-tellers. We all have to live by art, it's our daily bread – by what our language gives us, by what we invent for ourselves, by what we steal from others. And we should thank the gods for great artists who draw away the veil of anxiety and selfishness and show us, even for a moment, another world, a real world, and tell us a little bit of truth. And we should not be too hard on ourselves for being comforted by art.

ACASTOS

Hear, hear!

CALLISTOS *teasing Plato*

Give in, give in!

Plato laughs. The gathering is beginning to break up.

ACASTOS

You spoke of Eros. Don't you think that – on that *path* – that way – whether we can ever reach the end of it or not – that just loving each other – I mean loving as we love – and not only as lovers – is something that is – wonderful and – perhaps teaches most of all?

PLATO

Human love is so selfish.

CALLISTOS
Plato won't love until he has become a god and can love another god!

PLATO *to Acastos, laughingly*
Yes, yes, of course – you are right.

They all laugh, touching each other.

MANTIAS
You should go into politics, young fellow. You could go far. Come round to my place some time, we'll talk about it.

Callistos, who has been putting his mask on again, sees his chance and leaps up onto a table and begins to recite.

CALLISTOS
Zeus whoever he may be
If he cares to bear this name
By it I will clamour to
Zeus – no other can I see
To lift from soul the sullen weight,
But only he, who writes in thought
His fierce decree
That wisdom must be bought by pain.
As the slow ache comes again
Dripping grief on sleeping men,
So will wisdom come unsought
To those who never wanted to be taught.

Plato listens in anguish, tries to cover his ears. The others smile, allowing themselves to be moved by the poetry. At last Plato rushes at Callistos and drags him down and pulls the mask off.

PLATO
Oh stop – stop –

CALLISTOS
Don't be so rough!

DEXIMENES
Envy – envy – Plato knows he will never be a great poet.

PLATO
I'm going to destroy all my poems – tonight – I'll tear them up!

SOCRATES
Now, now, my children, be at peace, and don't tear things up, especially not poems. Our talk has moved under its own laws to a conclusion and has left us many things to talk about on another day. Let me thank you all – Deximenes, I thank you for your hospitality and this excellent and inspiring wine, I thank Mantias for so generously holding back his argument, I thank Acastos for being so certain that art is truth – and I thank Plato, who is youngest, for producing such a great shower of hazy, golden thoughts.

CALLISTOS
What about me?

SOCRATES
I thank you for being the most beautiful.

MANTIAS
I think he did very well.

DEXIMENES
You are the most beautiful, Socrates.

SOCRATES
And let us thank the gods for the gift of love, which Acastos spoke so truly of just now, and thank the god who *is* love, whom Plato praised with so much poetic eloquence. In truly loving each other we learn more perhaps than in all our other studies.

Laughing and embracing each other they begin to go away.
Plato and Socrates are last.

PLATO
Oh –

SOCRATES
What?

PLATO
I'm so happy. I don't know why. I love you so much.

SOCRATES
I'm so glad, Come – and – dear boy –

PLATO
Yes?

SOCRATES
Don't write it all down!

Plato laughs. Socrates puts his arm round
him and leads him off.

ABOVE THE GODS
A Dialogue about Religion

Characters in order of appearance

A SERVANT

ANTAGORAS   *a sophist, in love with Timonax*

TIMONAX   *a socially conscious youth*

ACASTOS   *a serious questing youth*

SOCRATES

PLATO

ALCIBIADES

Athens in the late fifth century B.C.

Socrates is about sixty years old, Alcibiades about forty, Plato about twenty.

Acastos, Antagoras and Timonax are fictional characters.

At the house of Antagoras. The servant is arranging wine and fruit. Enter, garlanded after a religious festival, Antagoras, Timonax and Acastos. Acastos smiles at the servant, who bows and withdraws. They fiddle with their garlands.

ACASTOS
I love religious festivals, they're such fun.

TIMONAX
Fun?

ACASTOS
Well, of course it's serious, it's a solemn occasion –

TIMONAX
I thought you didn't believe in fun!

ANTAGORAS
Religious people always have to pretend they enjoy it, it's their least elegant form of hypocrisy!

TIMONAX
Let's have a drink.

Enter Socrates. They all rise and wait till he is seated. They sit. Antagoras pulls Timonax to sit with him.

SOCRATES   *to Antagoras*
How kind of you to invite us.

ANTAGORAS
My house is honoured.

SOCRATES
Where's young Plato?

TIMONAX
Please not Plato, he's so emotional, he always spoils the
argument, he gets cross when he can't explain his ideas.

ACASTOS
My garland is full of fleas!

TIMONAX
So is mine!

Hasty removal of garlands.

ANTAGORAS
They recycle these things. What an image of human life,
flowers full of fleas!

ACASTOS   *watching the fleas with sympathy*
Ah, look at them!

ANTAGORAS
Animal lover!

SOCRATES
Acastos, did I hear you say you thought the festival was fun,
and then you felt you had to say it was 'a solemn occasion'?

TIMONAX
Off we go!

SOCRATES
Did you mean to contradict yourself? Ought we all to have had
long faces?

ACASTOS   *tense*
No. Yes. Perhaps we should. People were laughing and playing
about.

TIMONAX
Including you.

ANTAGORAS
Horse play. Our people have no dignity.

TIMONAX
It was a holiday!

SOCRATES   *to Acastos*
You disapprove?

ACASTOS
I *think* I disapprove. I mean, it's not *just* a holiday, we're
supposed to be honouring the gods.

ANTAGORAS
You don't believe in the gods.

ACASTOS
Well – yes, I do –

TIMONAX
Come off it, Acastos!

ACASTOS
In a way – sort of – I believe in *religion.*

SOCRATES
Can we distinguish religion from belief in gods?

Enter Plato. He clicks his heels and bows to Socrates.

ACASTOS
Oh, Plato, hello. Here – [*indicating a place beside him*]

TIMONAX
Do you believe in the gods, Plato?

Plato ignores him, sits beside Acastos.

Plato's garland's full of fleas. Why don't you wash sometimes?

ACASTOS
They all are!

Plato, irritated, unamused, removes his garland and tosses it away.

TIMONAX
Plato –

ANTAGORAS
Shut up.

SOCRATES   *to Antagoras*
May I suggest we celebrate this holy day by talking about religion? [*Antagoras bows assent.*] When I was young I was privileged to hear Zeno and Parmenides discussing religion –

ANTAGORAS
Those were godlike men!

SOCRATES
I was struck by their humility in the face of this awesome subject. So let us lesser beings be humble too. Suppose we start from a personal confession, that seems right when we speak of what is supposed to concern the individual soul. Tell me, Antagoras, do you believe in the gods?

ANTAGORAS
No, of course not! That's all fable, superstitious belief in the supernatural, mythology, suitable for childish primitives.

SOCRATES
Quite a lot of educated people believe in gods.

ANTAGORAS
Yes, but fewer and fewer, it's all going out. This is a time of transition. Our civilisation is growing up, we're scientific and factual, we can analyse the old superstitions and see how they

arose. God is not the measure of all things, man is the measure of all things, we invented the gods.

SOCRATES
Why? Why did we invent the gods?

ANTAGORAS
Well, originally out of fear of nature, fear of thunder for instance, people thought it was Zeus being angry. Religion is essentially magic, a desire for power over hostile forces. 'Religious experience' is just a comfortable feeling that the gods know all about us, there's a higher sense to it all, the gods have fixed the meaning of everything, so nothing is really dreadful or accidental or –

SOCRATES
You don't believe in divine spiritual beings?

ANTAGORAS
No! And if there were such beings *we* would be their *judges*. Any god who *existed* would be just a thing in our world, which *we* could decide about. It's not that God *must* exist, or *might* exist, it's that he can't *exist*. *We* are the source of morality and rational judgement. Once we understand this we *can't* believe in gods. We can't go back once we've become rational and free, it's an irreversible move.

SOCRATES
We are the gods now?

ANTAGORAS
Yes, if you like. The gods were just ideal pictures of us; we have to get rid of them to realise our own possibilities.

SOCRATES
The old philosophers, whom we think of as so wise, I mean like Thales and Heraclitus, saw the whole cosmos as a sort of

spiritual being, everything was holy, religion was a harmony with the whole of nature.

ANTAGORAS

Yes, but that was really science. They wanted to find out what the universe was made of, atoms and so on. Myth was mixed up with science in those days. Those were great men in their time but we've moved on.

SOCRATES

So religion is magic and primitive science – and primitive morality too? Since we've now discovered that we are the only source of value.

ANTAGORAS

Yes, religion has always been concerned with morals and social conduct, that's why it's been so important.

SOCRATES

Important?

ANTAGORAS

An important phenomenon. Morality was mixed up with mythology like science was, it was all one big thing, now we cut the thing into three pieces, throw away the mythology, and have a proper science and a proper morality. You must approve of that!

SOCRATES

What's 'proper'?

ANTAGORAS

More pure, more true, not mixed up with lies. Now we can *separate fact from value*, give each its proper place in life, get rid of the supernatural on both sides. Instead of cosmic mythology we have science, instead of picturesque god fables, we have independent moral men making up their minds and choosing their values. *We* are the lords of meaning, there isn't any higher meaning set up somewhere else. There's nothing high, there's nothing deep, there's nothing hidden – but that is *obvious*, it's what everybody in this room believes.

SOCRATES
Don't be impatient with me. I am not at all sure what everybody in this room believes. Not all intelligent people think that religion is just superstition. For instance someone might say that the old stories are not literally true, but that they can *convey* truth – and that there are not many gods but only one, called, perhaps, Zeus, or God, a spiritual power, which is perfectly good –

ANTAGORAS
Whether you call it Zeus or God or anything, it's still a supernatural person with a name and modern people can't believe in such a person.

SOCRATES
Can there be religion without gods or a personal god?

ANTAGORAS
No. Religion is *essentially* superstition.

SOCRATES
But has been closely connected with morality.

ANTAGORAS
People thought the gods would punish them for being bad and reward them for being good. A pretty debased sort of morality! Surely *you*, Socrates, would say that virtue is for its own sake and not for a reward!

SOCRATES
Let's go slowy. In philosophy if you aren't moving at a snail's

pace you aren't moving at all. Perhaps inside that connection with morality we may find many different things wrapped up.

ACASTOS
A pious superstitious peasant could be a better man than I am.

ANTAGORAS *quickly*
I wonder if you really believe that, Acastos? Superstitious belief is degrading, it's corrupting, it prevents thought, it's the acceptance of a lie.

SOCRATES
So you think religion is over, finished by the age of science. And this is a good thing?

ANTAGORAS
Well, yes – *and* no – Now this is *quite* another argument, it's a *political* argument. We intellectuals, we understand the situation, we can bear the burden –

SOCRATES
Of being gods.

ANTAGORAS
Of freedom and value and a responsible unaided morality. But considered simply as a social phenomenon religion can be a useful stabilising factor. We're living in a period of intellectual and psychological *shock*, a time of deep change, an interregnum, a *dangerous interim*. Public morality could break down, some would say it *is* breaking down.

SOCRATES
If you were a tyrant you wouldn't abolish religion?

ANTAGORAS
Not until I had found a substitute! Of course as you know I detest tyrants. But if people worshipped the gods and kept

quiet this might save the state from worse things. So long as there's an uneducated mob, there's a place for something like religion. Personally, I don't like the smell of it, religiosity is in bad taste, 'religious experience' is infantile fantasy; it's a matter of style. But this doesn't mean one should disrupt society to put people right. Religious sanctions, even rather vague ones, support popular morality and social order. Let's face it, ordinary morals are full of superstition, fear of the gods, fear of your neighbour, fear of the state. When young people lose that fear and become fearless, when they lose all respect for authority, things can really fall apart. It's a dangerous time. Religion is ritual and ritual is a symbol of order. Religion carries moral tradition. It's dying a natural and inevitable death, but the majority of people are slow in growing up. Meanwhile the state may have to take the place of the gods. [*Looking at Timonax.*] It's this *transition* that we intellectuals must try to *think* about. And we mustn't let sentimental modern political attitudes stop us from thinking.

During Antagoras's increasingly passionate speech Timonax has become extremely restive. He now bursts out.

TIMONAX
This is cynicism, it's elitism – !

ANTAGORAS
Public morality needs a popular background.

TIMONAX
I agreed with you before, but this –!

ANTAGORAS
Something with a bit of *colour* in it –

TIMONAX
You mean military parades!

ANTAGORAS
People must have faith in their society. Nationalism, patriotism, why not? Those are natural emotions.

TIMONAX
I shall go mad!

ANTAGORAS
The deification of the state is being forced upon us. I don't like it – but the alternative is anarchy!

By this time Antagoras, who is almost shouting, is thoroughly upset by his own logic, and Timonax is angry. Socrates makes pacifying gestures.

SOCRATES
This is indeed a new argument, a *political* argument about means to an end, means to a stable and orderly society. I think our original argument is more fundamental because it relates to values which can put political means and ends into question.

TIMONAX
He despises the morality of ordinary people, he thinks he's got a superior morality which justifies him treating them as puppets!

SOCRATES   *with a gesture towards Antagoras*
This would bring us back to Acastos's question about the superstitious but virtuous peasant. Is there not such a person?

ANTAGORAS
He might be virtuous but not in respect of his superstition.

SOCRATES
It's not so easy to separate a good man from his superstition. Might not someone who delayed his decision by praying to a god, come to a wiser decision?

ANTAGORAS

I prefer rational thought!

SOCRATES

You say this is a time of transition. Religious dogma is also changing. Could there not be a good religious way of life without the supernatural beliefs?

ACASTOS *vigorously nodding assent to this question*

Yes!

ANTAGORAS

I wouldn't call that religion. I see what you are at, Socrates, but I won't let you do it. You want to smuggle religion back as some sort of refined morality. I shouldn't have allowed you and Acastos to posit this virtuous peasant, and I won't let my political argument be undercut by your moral argument. I don't believe in goodness in your grand solemn sense. I don't believe in moral perfectionism. Morality is a profoundly relative matter, the concept is irremediably confused, it's not something glorious and eternal, *that's what we've learnt from* getting rid of the gods! *If we go beyond the simplest ideas about morality we land in nonsense.* Philosophers always try to invent some impressive background or 'underlying reality'. But morality has no background except the actual continuance of human society, it's practically important, but in a theoretical sense it's a superficial phenomenon. *There isn't anything deep or high.* You want to separate out a part of religion to do with perfect virtue or salvation or something, to make religion go on existing without supernatural beliefs, but there is no such part. We're all the same, only some of us are more rational and free. Anything else is pure hypocrisy!

SOCRATES

My dear Antagoras, please don't be cross with me. You imagine I am up to all kinds of trickery, I assure you I am not. I am simply trying to hold onto the strands of what has already become quite a complicated argument. Do you mind if we now let Timonax join in? He has been bursting to for some time.

ANTAGORAS
He won't be happy until he's attacking me, he's such a pugnacious boy. But he won't agree with you either.

TIMONAX *incoherent with annoyance and conviction, to Antagoras*
It's nothing to do with *you*, it isn't *personal*, it's a matter of *truth* and – and how things *are* – you deny morality –

ANTAGORAS *cooler*
I don't, I just define it in a modest manner.

TIMONAX
But you take a high moral line when it suits you! Socrates seems to want religion to go on as virtue or something –

ACASTOS
Socrates hasn't said –

TIMONAX
And you want it to go on as a drug to stop people from resisting tyranny –

ANTAGORAS
No, I don't –

SOCRATES
Stop, let him talk.

TIMONAX *very fast*
Of *course* the old stories are lies, but they're lies that have got to be *destroyed*. Religion is *immoral*, it stops people from thinking about how to change society. Yes, we are at the end of our childhood, and we must get rid of that old primitive past

and *kick* it to *pieces*. I think *men* should be gods, not the state. I happen to believe in democracy and that means making *everybody* capable of thinking and distinguishing true and false. I believe in brotherhood and equality and all those things which modern science makes possible at last. Religion has always been a reactionary force, it makes people lazy and stupid, it consoles them for their rotten lives, they can think about heaven and not care about changing the world –

ANTAGORAS
I'm all for changing the world, I just think it can't be done in ten days!

TIMONAX
You're a cynic!

ANTAGORAS
I'm a pragmatist.

TIMONAX
Your pragmatism leads straight into tyranny, you say religiosity is in bad taste, you say morality is a matter of style –

ANTAGORAS   *under Timonax's flow*
I don't –

TIMONAX
You say there's nothing deep and nothing high, but there is, *truth* is, and *caring about people* is, morality *matters*, it isn't relative, it's absolute, we can't be *relaxed* about all this. Religion is false, it's degrading, it makes real morality impossible, now for the first time we can have *real* morality which is just for itself. If we're gods we must be good truthful gods and make society more moral and good, and another thing, religion isn't just dream stuff, it's a political force, it commits terrible crimes, intolerance and persecution and cruelty, it's like a

political party, it *is* a political party, and even people who don't
believe in religion are sentimental about it. Religious leaders
may have lots of charm, what everyone now calls 'charisma', I
hate that word, but look what they *do*, they interfere with
social arrangements and tell us what to do in our private lives,
and what we can *read*, they even prevent their own thinkers
from thinking –

ANTAGORAS
If you imagine that all religious leaders are hypocrites you are
being dangerously naive.

TIMONAX
You don't deny that the Delphic Oracle is a political fraud, do
you? Do you, Acastos?

ACASTOS
No.

TIMONAX
Religion is the enemy of morality, anything that rests on lies
must be, the basis of morality is making people happier and
freer and better, more equal, more tolerant, more truthful,
more just, that's *absolutely* important, and it's as high and as
deep as you please, that's what I mean by *idealism*. Who
disagrees with that?

Timonax has by now risen to his feet in his excitement.
Acastos is upset and confused.

SOCRATES
Perhaps we shall agree that these are moral *aims*, but this is not
to say that such aims are the *basis* or *definition* of morality.
And, dear Timonax, please sit down, your eloquence is making
me feel quite tired. You see, we are in deep waters. Antagoras
and Timonax seem to be agreeing about religion but differing

about morality. If, as Antagoras put it, there is 'nothing high and nothing deep' this takes away an important part of the traditional conception of religion, that part which *connects morality* with some absolute background. Antagoras also of course denies the absolute status which Timonax gives to morals.

ANTAGORAS
Timonax contradicts himself, he is taking up a religious attitude, his 'absolute' is just God, it can't be anything else!

SOCRATES   *to Timonax, who has dismissed this remark with a derisive gesture*
Do you want to add anything now?

TIMONAX
No, but I shall speak again if I hear anybody talking nonsense.

SOCRATES
I'm sure you will, dear boy. Now let's hear a different voice, I suspect there's one not far off. Plato? [*Plato shakes his head slightly.*] Acastos, I think it's your task to help us now. [*Acastos makes a helpless gesture.*] Never mind if you've nothing clear to say, just try to say your unclear thing as directly as possible.

ACASTOS
I agree with lots of things they said, I don't believe in the old myths and stories, and of course religion does a lot of bad things –

SOCRATES
But – ?

ACASTOS
I suppose it's a silly argument, but all those people who

believed in religion for so long can't just have been mistaken, I mean it's not a bit like an ordinary factual mistake.

SOCRATES

It's not necessarily easy to say what an ordinary factual mistake is. Our whole way of seeing the world is changing exceptionally fast.

ACASTOS

Yes, we've found out *hundreds* of things, like what people in the past would never have dreamt of –

SOCRATES

And might not all these new methods of explanation affect our whole outlook, change our perspective, so that now we simply *can't* believe things which people did in the past? Religion is a mode of explanation, it explained the world, it guaranteed morality, it made it all look *real*. Now our sense of reality has shifted, we explain the world in new ways which cohere with all our new knowledge.

ACASTOS

Yes, it all looked so solid and impressive *then* and doesn't *now*. We have science and – and morality is [*touches his chest*] our own judgement – I suppose – I'm not clear about that. And the whole atmosphere is getting anti-religious as if religion couldn't breathe any more. We know so much – but not about ourselves – we're so – each one of us – so *amazing* [*expressive gestures*] – I mean more amazing than the stars, or anything – and we seem to *need* something – there's a part of us that *wants* –

TIMONAX

Wants God!

ANTAGORAS
Illusions, dear child.

ACASTOS
Well, people like to feel that they can talk to God – but religion can't be slavish subjection to some supernatural person, it's got to be freely accepted.

SOCRATES
There is a saying of Heraclitus that 'he who alone is wise wants and does not want to be called Zeus.' What do you think that means?

ACASTOS *with gestures*
I think it means that we're drawn to the idea of a sort of central – good – something very real – after all morality *feels* more like discovering something than just inventing it – and we want to sort of *assert* this central thing – by giving it a *name* – but at the same time we see this is wrong, it makes it like a material thing, we can't conceive it in this way, and it's as if it itself forbids us to.

SOCRATES
Yes, truth forbids what also seems a natural even inevitable way of formulating something important. We put the truth into a conceptual picture because we feel it can't be expressed in any other way; and then truth itself forces us to criticise the picture.

Slight pause.

Is this unusual? Isn't it rather like what artists are doing all the time?

ACASTOS
You mean using images, and then trying to improve them, and –

SOCRATES

In a way we are all artists, we all use metaphors and symbols and figures of speech, and we can't always explain what they mean in other terms, any more than we can with a work of art. We're surrounded by statues and pictures of gods and stories about them. Religion has always used art, and art has helped to make the mythology look so real. But at times religion has also rejected art, and perhaps it's doing so now. Do you want religion to go on existing?

ACASTOS

Yes, but not with lying. Yet I feel that if we lose traditional religion now we may lose *all* religion because – it can't use the old language and concepts – and it can't make new ones in time – and many people find it empty and senseless – and then when the priests change the old-fashioned language into modern words it sounds so ugly and awkward, it loses its spiritual force – it's as if the gods can't speak to us any more, they are silent, they've hidden themselves. But I don't want worship and ritual and prayer and so on just to *go* – there's a valuable – precious – thing somewhere inside it all.

SOCRATES

Well, that's the thing that we want to find.

ANTAGORAS

Your precious thing is just a dream of morality. Morality with flowers round its neck and fleas in the flowers.

ACASTOS

No, no – religion is having an intense attitude and no time off. [*Laughter, in which Plato does not join.*] I mean, it's *more* like life, like *real* life. Life is awful, terrible, like in war, and we're always at war, and then death comes to us all and – religion is about those awful deep things.

ANTAGORAS
There's nothing deep, Acastos, that's the message of the modern world and we've got to live with it!

ACASTOS
Religion is – something that stays put when you're terribly unhappy or – guilty. It's like being sure that in spite of all evil – and selfishness – and pain – there really is goodness, and that it matters – more than anything else – all the time and everywhere, and it's true – more than our ordinary – dreamy life – and so morality isn't just what we happen to think – it's like discovering the truth, or remembering it.

TIMONAX
But religious people think they're going to live for ever in heaven!

ACASTOS
We can't know that, so it has nothing to do with us. I think immortality is an anti-religious idea, as if there were rewards or anything happening somewhere else. It's all got to be *now* and *here*.

ANTAGORAS
What has?

ACASTOS
That sort of – absolute seriousness.

TIMONAX
But that *is* morality.

ANTAGORAS
Religion is just morality plus a tragic feeling.

ACASTOS
No! [*voices raised*]

SOCRATES
Wait, wait! I want Acastos to tell us how he thinks religion
relates to morality. Some people might say that morality is just
public social rules and that there are a lot of serious private
things which have nothing whatever to do with morals. Would
you say that, Timonax?

TIMONAX   *after a moment's reflection*
Yes, so long as that doesn't make morality unimportant.

SOCRATES   *to Acastos*
And isn't that a sensible view, isn't that common sense?

ANTAGORAS
It's certainly *political* common sense!

ACASTOS
I think religion *contains* morality. It goes beyond common
sense, it goes beyond that sort of limited attitude, dividing the
world into manageable bits. Religion is believing that your life
is a *whole* – I mean that goodness and morality and duty are
just *everywhere* – like *always* looking further and deeper – and
feeling *reverence* for things – a religious person would care
about everything in that sort of way, he'd feel everything
mattered and every second mattered.

SOCRATES
No time off!

TIMONAX
Oh come, you must draw the line somewhere!

SOCRATES
Perhaps for Acastos religion means not drawing the line.

ACASTOS
That's what one would mean by saying that Zeus is always
watching.

TIMONAX
You don't believe that Zeus is always watching!

ACASTOS
No, I mean it's *as if*! It's like we're [*expressive gesture*] *immersed*.

ANTAGORAS
'All is one' is the oldest lie in the philosophy book.

SOCRATES   *while Acastos nods*
So a religious attitude sees our life as an interconnected whole and a religious man would feel responsible for the *quality* of all his thoughts and experiences, even his perceptions, as if everything were significant and worthy of justice?

ACASTOS
Yes, this sort of – *perpetual work* – seems to me what religion is.

SOCRATES
You approve of such an attitude?

ACASTOS
Yes, it's – as I see it – it's like – it's humility and unselfishness – and setting yourself aside to make room for other things, and people –

TIMONAX
But you can't care about everything, that's a ridiculous conceited idea, not a bit humble, anyway you'd go mad! You're talking about states of mind all the time, lofty private emotions, what about actions, actions are what matter –

ACASTOS
I don't mean *just* emotions – actions come out of states of mind and how we *see* the world, we can only move in the world we

can see, we have to change ourselves and become better and understand more –

ANTAGORAS
We can't change ourselves, we've always known that, only now we know why!

SOCRATES
You said religion contained morality. Do you want to say that religion is the *basis* of morality?

ACASTOS   *obviously exhausted by his ordeal*
I don't know. Lots of religious people are bad and lots of non-religious people are good.

SOCRATES
Does that tend to disprove your position?

ACASTOS
I don't think so.

SOCRATES
You've done very well, Acastos, but you haven't told us how to distinguish between morality and religion. Perhaps religion is just a 'refined' sort of morality which some people choose to invent?

TIMONAX
Neurotic people!

ACASTOS
Well, part of it is that you don't invent it, it's absolutely *there*, like a – *judgement*.

SOCRATES
Now gather yourself together for a final assault.

ACASTOS   *struggling*
I can't –

SOCRATES
Can there be religion without mythology, without stories and pictures? Should we be trying now to think of it like that?

ACASTOS
I don't know!

SOCRATES
Is a certain opaqueness, a certain *mystery*, necessary to it?

ACASTOS   *almost tearful*
I don't know!

SOCRATES
Would you say that religion is something *natural*?

TIMONAX
Socrates, do stop, let's have an interval, let's drink and not think! Acastos says there is no time off from religion, but do let's have some time off from philosophy!

Socrates relaxes and smiles, signs assent.

ANTAGORAS
When it gets difficult he wants a drink.

TIMONAX
I *love* arguing!

ANTAGORAS
Only when you win.

TIMONAX
Socrates, defend me.

SOCRATES   *petting him*
One who is so beautiful needs no other defence.

ANTAGORAS
I think we should go on, otherwise we'll lose the thread, we'll

lose the *intensity*, to use Acastos's favourite word. [*He claps his hands for the servant.*]

TIMONAX   *pleasantly*
Acastos isn't religious, he's just a prig, aren't you, dear?

The servant enters bringing more wine.
Typical behaviour of each character to him. Socrates is relaxed and amiable, Acastos would-be friendly but awkward, Timonax perfunctory, Antagoras indifferent. Plato observes and frowns.

TIMONAX   *indicating the servant*
Well, if you want to go on and we want to rest why not question this chap? I know Socrates never needs a rest.

SOCRATES
What does Antagoras think?

ANTAGORAS
Whatever you like. He's not very bright and he can't speak the language very well.

As they discuss the servant Acastos is uncomfortable, looks at Plato who remains impassive.

TIMONAX
Has he got a religion?

ANTAGORAS
I don't know, better ask him.

SOCRATES
I would like Acastos to question him.

ACASTOS
Oh no, please not!

SOCRATES
I won't always be here to ask questions, others must learn.
Besides you are young and gentle and won't upset him. Go on,
my dear.

ACASTOS *nervous*
We're talking about religion. [*It takes a moment for him to
attract the servant's attention*] Look – excuse me –

ANTAGORAS
He lives in a dream. He isn't even listening.

ACASTOS
Do you have a *religion?*

SERVANT
A what, sir? No, I don't think so, sir.

The servant is a graceful youth. He is a little timid at first.

TIMONAX
That shows it isn't natural.

SOCRATES
Tell him what it is.

ACASTOS
Oh dear – I mean when you go to services, rituals, acts of
worship.

SERVANT
I don't know what is that –

SOCRATES
Don't use difficult words.

ACASTOS
When you sing hymns, you sing –

SERVANT *cheering up*
Oh, yes, sing hymns, yes, and music, noise, yes, beat, your heart
beat, and your feet – [*He moves a few steps.*]

ACASTOS *as they all smile*
So you believe in God, you think that perhaps there is a God?

SERVANT
Oh no –

TIMONAX
Fun, but no God. Hooray!

SERVANT
Not like that – I don't think – I *know* there is God.

ANTAGORAS
Ask him what he's like.

ACASTOS
What is your God like?

SERVANT
I don't understand. *Everybody* knows that, sir.

ANTAGORAS
Well, we don't, so please tell us.

ACASTOS *with an encouraging gesture*
Go on.

SERVANT
How can I say, he is everywhere, he knows all things, he made
all things, he is God, he is here in this room –

ANTAGORAS
I can't see him. [*Socrates checks him with a gesture.*]

ACASTOS
How do you know about God?

SERVANT
I have always known, sir, ever since I was a tiny baby, my first
words were about God. I knew him at once.

ACASTOS
You mean your mother taught you?

SERVANT
My mother – [*assenting gesture*] but I know it already, he was
there, in my little body, in all I see when I open my eyes, when I
was a child, and now, in my heart and my soul – so is God in all
men.

ACASTOS
And you worship God.

SERVANT
I don't know – He is with me always, I sing to him, I laugh to
him, I cry to him. And when I die I shall go to God. That makes
me happy. Whatever happen, I am happy man.

TIMONAX
Lucky old you!

ACASTOS
You pray to God sometimes?

SERVANT *scornful*
Not sometimes, all the time! I talk to him, I tell him my life, I tell
him all troubles, all what I want.

ACASTOS
Does he give you what you want?

SERVANT
He knows best, oh he knows best. He knows what is my good. I
am humble man, small man. But God blesses me.

ACASTOS
So you love him because he is kind?

SERVANT
Not therefore! I love him because he is God. Even if he kill me, I love him. I love him more than anything, not anybody more I love than God.

ACASTOS
But why?

SERVANT *who thinks this is obvious*
He loves me, he made me to be, he keeps me to be. Like little fish in sea am I in God's love! All I eat, sleep, work, do, inside his love. Because I exist there is God. Without his love I become small like – like this – and wither away, and become – no thing [*gestures*].

ANTAGORAS
Gift of language these fellows have.

TIMONAX
Don't you ever pray to God to make you rich and grand, like him? [*He points to Antagoras.*]

SERVANT
I am well off man inside God's love, that is all I know.

TIMONAX
I don't believe you. Aren't you cross with God because he made you like this?

SERVANT *upset*
I am not good man, I have many sin, many fault, many, many. I need my God. I am all bad, he is all good, I have bad thoughts –

TIMONAX *interrupting*
So if you –

SOCRATES *stopping the conversation with a gesture*
Thank you, thank you, you spoke very well.

At a nod from Antagoras the servant goes. Socrates rises and stands a little apart.

ANTAGORAS
I suppose he's what they call a natural mystic!

ACASTOS
So you *do* think religion is natural?

ANTAGORAS
Superstition is! He believes it all literally.

TIMONAX
Whatever happen I am happy man. Perhaps *that's* religion.

ACASTOS
I liked that!

TIMONAX
No wonder it inhibits social progress!

ANTAGORAS
I was afraid he was going to confess he'd stolen something, most embarrassing!

TIMONAX
With God standing there looking at him accusingly!

ANTAGORAS
There you are, not a bad idea if it stops people from stealing!

TIMONAX
He's rather adorable, would you sell him to me!

ANTAGORAS
What do you want him for?

Socrates returns to the group and stands in front of Plato,
studying him. Plato is uneasy, rises, moves. The others watch.

SOCRATES
Well, what do you think, young Plato? We don't seem to have
heard from you.

PLATO *after a moment, cool, almost impertinent*
Do you really want to know what I think?

They stare at each other. Then Socrates turns away and sits
down, beckoning to Acastos. They are all seated except for
Plato who is left out.

SOCRATES *to Acastos*
Well, my child, we are still without a definition of religion
which separates it clearly from morality.

ACASTOS
I think that —

PLATO *vehemently interrupting, very fast*
Religion isn't just a feeling, it isn't just a hypothesis, it's not like
something we happen not to know, a God who might perhaps
be there isn't a God, it's got to be necessary, it's got to be
certain, it's got to be proved by the whole of life, it's got to be
the magnetic centre of everything —

SOCRATES
Wait a minute! So you want to talk?

PLATO
Yes. [*pause*] Please.

SOCRATES
All right. Sit down. And don't be in such a hurry. You say 'it's
got to be certain.' There are different kinds of certainty.

TIMONAX
Intolerance, dogmatism, persecution.

SOCRATES
And what is one to be certain of? You used the word God.

PLATO *still fast*
That was just a figure of speech, of course there are no gods, they are just images, religion is above the gods, there *can't* be gods, but that doesn't mean it's anything we happen to think, it doesn't mean *we're* the gods, that's just the *opposite*, it's beyond us, it's more real than us, we have to come to it and let it change us, religion is spiritual change, *absolute* spiritual change.

SOCRATES
Not so fast please. Moral ideals can change people too.

PLATO
Not so deeply, not in the way that's *required* of us, this isn't something optional, we're not volunteers, we're conscripts. We're bad, we have to become good, it's a long way. Anyhow morality, if it's anything serious, is something religious.

SOCRATES
Whether it knows it or not?

PLATO
Yes. I mean, what I'd *call* religion is what can really *change* us. Morality is derivative, it's a shadow of religion, the gods are shadows of religion, *we* are shadows, looking for the light, looking for the sun, for what's *real* and *necessarily* true.

SOCRATES
Many people would say that *necessity* belongs to mathematics and logic. In the real world things aren't necessarily true, they may or may not be true, we have to look and see.

PLATO
That's just where religion is *different*, it's unique, it's about what's *absolute*, what *can't* not be there. If we conceive it at all we see that it must be real.

SOCRATES
What is this 'it' that you're certain of in this special unique way, which isn't God and which has to exist and is proved by everything and is seen in the clear light beyond the shadows?

PLATO
Good.

ANTAGORAS
What did he say?

PLATO
Good.

TIMONAX
That's an abstract idea.

ANTAGORAS
It's an empty box into which we put whatever takes our fancy.

SOCRATES
By 'good' do you mean virtue?

PLATO
Virtue under a necessity to which everything points. I mean – to become virtuous is the absolute goal of human life –

ANTAGORAS
Oh – ! [*Derisive moan*]

PLATO   *ignoring him*
But we can't switch it on by empty will power. We have to *learn* what's true and what's real and that *is* understanding and

loving what's good, that's how *everything* teaches us, everything *proves* it —

SOCRATES
Wait — Timonax said that good is an abstract idea, and Antagoras called it an empty box. Perhaps what they meant is that it must leave us *free* to call *all* sorts of things good.

PLATO
I don't think freedom is very important.

ACASTOS
Oh really! [*Timonax and Antagoras also exclaim.*]

PLATO
Choosing just anything you like —

ANTAGORAS
That's *political* freedom and it *is* important.

PLATO
Real spiritual freedom is very difficult. I'd rather give it some other name like — truth.

ACASTOS
Truth.

PLATO
Truth isn't just *facts*, it's a *mode of being.* It's finding out what's real and responding to it — like when we really see other people and know they exist. You see I think there are different levels in the soul, only a bit of us is real and knows truth, the rest is fantasy, anxiety, resentment, envy, all selfish tricks — *you* know. We live in a dream, we're wrapped up in a dark veil, we think we're omnipotent magicians, we don't believe anything *exists* except ourselves. Magic is the opposite of goodness. Belief in magic is slavery. We have to change ourselves, change

what we want, what we desire, what we love, and that's difficult. But if we even *try* to love what's good our desires can improve, they can change direction, *that's* what I call freedom. *That's* becoming morally better, and it's possible and that's *why* it's possible. Real freedom is not to be a slave of selfish desires. It's when you have – you know – a feeling of reality –

ACASTOS   *nodding, softly*
Yes.

ANTAGORAS
I never heard such high-minded rubbish! And I don't like this talk about 'the soul'!

PLATO
Well, the psyche then, a perfectly good Greek word!

ANTAGORAS
You mean we stop being individual people and vanish into a golden haze?

PLATO
No! We *become* individual people, and stop being self-absorbed mucky dreamers!

ACASTOS
Mucky dreamers –

PLATO
We become more real –

TIMONAX
You say 'love good'. How do we find out what *is* good?

PLATO
All truth-seeking teaches that, everybody knows something about it really –

SOCRATES

You connect goodness with truth-seeking and knowledge. But mightn't we just be idle spectators of what we know, why should it affect what we do?

PLATO

That's where love and desire come in, what Acastos left out. Think of what learning something is like, something difficult like mathematics. You know how that feels when you're trying so hard to see something which *isn't yourself*, something *else*. You forget yourself. All your being and emotions are involved in trying to *understand*, and that's the sort of *desire* that actions come out of too, when you can't help responding because you really care.

SOCRATES

You choose an intellectual example, but it needn't be intellectual learning, it could be a craft.

PLATO

Almost anything – like carpentry – when the carpenter begins to understand, to *see*, to learn some mathematics. [*Turning to Antagoras*] *That's* deep.

SOCRATES

Or learning about other people, you do what's right when you've forgotten yourself and really understand them.

PLATO

Learning other people, that's much harder. What's easiest is – is beauty – when you see beautiful things and just want them to exist outside, in themselves, so that you can love them and understand them. Beauty is a clue, it's the nearest thing, it's the only spiritual thing we love by instinct –

ANTAGORAS

What's all this got to do with religion?

PLATO

It *is* religion and it's happening all the time. If it's not everywhere, in the air we breathe, it isn't what I mean. If it's something whose non-existence is possible it isn't what I mean! It's to do with life being a whole and not a lot of random choices. Religion must be proved by the whole of life, it isn't a sort of oddity or side issue or one choice among others, it isn't weird like magic. If it's anything it must be everything, it must be proved by loving people and learning things and looking at things. It's not abstract, it's all *here*. It's not retiring from the world, it's knowing the world, the real world, *this* world as it really is, in all its – details –

TIMONAX

You mean *everything*, bits of hair, and mud, and dirt, and fleas and – ?

PLATO   [*after a moment*] Yes.

SOCRATES

But what about this 'learning other people', which is so difficult, and so important?

PLATO

Yes, we seem to be naturally good about beauty and bad about people.

TIMONAX

What about beautiful people, what about falling in love!

ANTAGORAS

Don't change the subject.

SOCRATES   *smiling*

He isn't changing the subject!

PLATO

Well, falling in love! It's suddenly as if you didn't exist any more, there's nothing in the world but the other person, all reality has gone somewhere else, he's like a god, it's the most violent experience we ever have —

SOCRATES
A good experience?

PLATO
It can be —

ANTAGORAS
It can be *hell.*

SOCRATES
Lovers are often jealous and selfish and cruel.

TIMONAX
Usually, in my experience.

PLATO
Yes, like when you want to *cage* the other person and *dominate* him and *crush* him — but I think falling in love is a sort of *picture* of something good. I mean *as if* one could love very much but without selfishness.

TIMONAX
Impossible.

SOCRATES
You mean one ought ideally to care for everybody in an unselfish way, even to love them. Perhaps the lover might learn to understand spiritual beauty as the carpenter learns to understand mathematics.

PLATO   *gradually becoming excited and rising to his feet*
We can't. And yet we can. We *can* change. You see, love is energy. The soul is a huge vast place, and lots of it is dark, and it's full of energy and power, and this can be bad, but it *can* be

good, and *that's* the *work*, to change bad energy into good, when we desire good things and are attracted magnetically by them –

ANTAGORAS
I think your magnetic Good isn't God after all, it's just sex, all this dark energy is sex.

PLATO
All right, it's sex, or sex is it – it's the whole drive of our being and that includes sex.

SOCRATES
Perhaps there is a god there after all. I would call him Eros.

PLATO
Eros! Yes!

SOCRATES
Only your Eros isn't exactly a god, he's a holy passionate spirit that seeks for God, what you call Good.

PLATO
Yes! He's *in love* with Good!

ANTAGORAS
But your Good is an *idea*.

SOCRATES
Do sit down, Plato!

PLATO   *sits*
Ideas *work* in life, they can become incarnate in how we live, that's how they become real!

ANTAGORAS
These are just attractive metaphors.

PLATO

Metaphors aren't just ornaments, they're fundamental modes of knowledge – it's like – what's at a higher more difficult level appears to us first as a shadow, or an image – then we break through the image and move on and –

SOCRATES

Like the carpenter learning mathematics. [*Plato nods*] But can we get beyond images and *see* your Good, which you said was like the sun?

PLATO

I don't know. In a way, goodness and truth seem to come out of the depths of the soul, and when we really know something we feel we've always known it. Yet also it's terribly distant, farther than any star. We're sort of – stretched out – It's like beyond the world, not in the clouds or in heaven, but a light that *shows* the world, this world, as it really is –

SOCRATES

You want your Good, your source of true light to be separate and pure and perfect –

PLATO

It's like what Acastos said when in spite of all wickedness, and in all misery, we are certain that there really *is* goodness and that it matters *absolutely*.

SOCRATES

But you wouldn't call it God.

PLATO

No, it's not a *person*, we don't have dialogues with it, it won't reward us, we must be good for nothing, it's an *idea*, it's the closest thing [*gesture*] –

SOCRATES
And the farthest thing.

ACASTOS
What about prayer? In your picture can we pray?

PLATO
Yes, but not to a person. Learning can be praying, breathing
can be praying. Prayer is keeping quiet and hoping for the light.

ANTAGORAS
Why should ultimate reality be something nice and good? It
might be something thoroughly nasty. Either your Good is a
thing existing outside us like God, or it's a picture inside us
which some people choose to play about with.

PLATO
Now *you're* using metaphors —

ANTAGORAS
What metaphors?

PLATO
Inside and outside! Of course Good doesn't exist like chairs
and tables, it's not [*gestures*] either outside or inside. It's in
our whole way of living, it's fundamental like truth. If we have
the idea of value we necessarily have the idea of perfection as
something real.

SOCRATES
So you think everybody knows this?

PLATO
Instinctively, yes. People know that good is real and absolute,
not optional and relative, all their life proves it. And when they
choose false goods they really know they're false. We can think
everything else away out of life, but not value, that's in the very
— ground of things.

ACASTOS   *to himself, thinking*
We can't think material objects away out of life – or can we? Or
causal connections? Or is that different?

SOCRATES
Is this where you distinguish morality from religion?

PLATO
Yes, except that I don't. Religion is the love and worship of the
good, and that's the real basis of morality. Duty, that's what we
feel when we want the good but love other things more –

SOCRATES
So some people are religious without knowing it? They
mightn't like that.

PLATO
I suppose so. I don't like the word 'religion' actually.

TIMONAX
So after all you're giving up?

PLATO
Nowadays people think of religion as something exotic and
formal, and a bit aside from life, whereas what I mean is
everywhere, like breathing.

SOCRATES   *thoughtfully*
Sometimes in philosophy we come up against questions which
we can't answer, as if our language were a cage and we were
right up against the bars. Acastos said he wanted religion to go
on, as if it might or mightn't go on. What you call the ground of
things, proved by everything, *if* it exists, is bound to go on, it
can't not. But how is it to be expressed? Even your phrase 'the
ground of being' or whatever is a metaphor which is understood in a tradition. Religion expressed this idea very strongly,
very picturesquely. Now it seems like something much harder

to explain, *you* find it hard to explain. Perhaps it needs new metaphors, a new way of thought. But that hasn't happened yet. People still think of religion in the old way, as something formal, with certain rituals, symbols, familiar pictures. You said religion was spiritual change. What changes people must reach their minds and their hearts. Can religion survive without a *mythology*? Perhaps the concept is simply breaking up? Concepts don't live for ever, you yourself said you didn't like the word 'religion'. Isn't that symptomatic?

PLATO
I don't know. I think of mythology as a whole set of false stories. Human life is coherent enough. There are *lots* of ways of talking about the – absolute – however you put it, with *true* images, *true* pointers, natural – sacraments – One thing can stand for another, that's as deep as what's deepest. People have always known this.

ACASTOS   *not expecting an answer*
So it's about what *ordinary* people can believe? It couldn't just be a secret – No, of course not.

SOCRATES
Your Good, your sun, your holy light shining from outside existent being and yet also emerging from deep inside the soul. Aren't these mythological pictures? Would you say it's *as if* this were so?

PLATO   *visibly tiring now*
Not 'as if'. Learning and loving just are *like that*!

SOCRATES
One way of describing the world, perhaps, not an obvious one?

PLATO
When you see things in that light –

SOCRATES
Another metaphor.

TIMONAX
Give up Plato, you're cornered!

SOCRATES
I don't think he's cornered!

PLATO *making a new move*
It's *got* to be like that otherwise we won't survive. The spirit must have something *absolute*, otherwise it goes crazy. Only religion can carry us through the – horrors – of the future –

SOCRATES
That's a different point. We've had plenty of horrors in the recent past – you think there are more to come?

PLATO
Yes.

SOCRATES
Then your 'ground of things', your 'it must be so', is really 'I want it to be so', it's a cry of fear?

PLATO
No –

SOCRATES
Perhaps you yourself are being too absolute. Religion naturally uses myth and art. These things too are instinctive, and perhaps religion will look after itself better than you imagine. You spoke of beauty – ritual is art, and art is the celebration of beauty. You say we're not gods. But you expect us as thinkers to *clarify* these things which must perhaps always be mysterious and even *fundamentally* muddled. You say spirit must have absolute. Perhaps we are now entering a time when *spirit cannot have any absolute.*

PLATO
Oh – *no* – but it will be different later?

SOCRATES
Who knows what will happen later [*pause*]. I like what you say, I love what you say and I love you as you say it.

PLATO
Don't you love me all the time?

SOCRATES
Yes, but especially in this. Now I want you to go on –

PLATO
I can't go on!

SOCRATES
My dear good clever boy, now just try quietly to tell us –

Enter Alcibiades drunk, supported by the servant. Alcibiades puts on a 'camp' manner, but must be seen to be a tough dominating figure, a soldier and a leader. He could be wearing some sort of uniform.

ALCIBIADES
Socrates! I've been looking for you all over. Darling!

SOCRATES   *obviously pleased to see him*
Alcibiades, come in, sit down. [*To Antagoras*] May he join us?

Antagoras makes a helpless humorous gesture.

ALCIBIADES   *to Socrates*
My *love*! He's blushing. Oh you sweet one! The wisest man in the world and he blushes like a boy! Hello, Antagoras, I see you've still got goldilocks, lucky you! And this pretty animal [*stroking the servant*], nice good animal! Oh *Plato*, written

any poems lately, dear? Love poems? [*Plato turns his head away.*] Oh sulky! What a sulky pussy! What have you been discussing?

During his speech Alcibiades has inserted himself into the group, sitting beside Socrates and causing the others to move up. A little horseplay, pulls Timonax's hair etc.

ANTAGORAS
Religion.

ALCIBIADES
My favourite subject!

SOCRATES
I imagine you wouldn't call yourself a religious man?

ANTAGORAS
Was it you who castrated all those statues of the gods?

ALCIBIADES
Ssssh! The gods deserve to be castrated. Who are they to flaunt their organs at us? But have you really been talking about *them?* [*pointing upwards*]

SOCRATES
I think we've passed beyond the gods. No one seems to want to defend them except me.

TIMONAX
Socrates!

ALCIBIADES
He's a deep one. We don't know how to have him! But where are we if we're beyond the gods?

SOCRATES
Plato has been telling us about being in love.

ALCIBIADES
My subject too!

TIMONAX
He's in love with Good.

ALCIBIADES
Is it mutual?

ANTAGORAS
He thinks that goodness is the same as knowledge.

ALCIBIADES
But I think that too!

PLATO   *tense, very hostile*
No, you don't. We can't possibly be agreeing. Religion is the
love and worship of goodness and truth, it's a magnetic power,
it's absolute, and if we really love what's good we become
good, and –

ALCIBIADES
Oh *Pusskins* –

PLATO
You're drunk!

SOCRATES
Let him say what he means. Come on, and *please* be serious.

ALCIBIADES
Oh, I am, it comes from the heart, to which dear Pusskins here
attaches such importance. I will tell you what religion is. It is
the love and worship of power.

PLATO
That's –

SOCRATES   *silencing Plato with a gesture*
Power?

ALCIBIADES
What is vulgarly called magic, but what I mean is something
deep, as deep as you please, as deep as Plato.

SOCRATES
You'll have to perform some magic yourself if you are to
persuade us that power is the object, or essence, of religion.

ALCIBIADES
Well, call it other names. Plato's very good at that, he's a
juggler, a magician, a little apprentice magician who had better
scuttle back to poetry and leave philosophy to stronger heads.
He says religion is the worship of the good, then he calls it truth
and knowledge, and it's magnetic and it's absolute and – it's all
done by mirrors – by *equations* which hang miraculously in the
air!

SOCRATES
Well, what are *your* other names, since you admit you can play
the game as well?

ALCIBIADES
The game is called me-ta-phy-sics. But about religion, surely
you are in the secret? I am sure Plato is, for all his priggish talk.

SOCRATES
Stop playing about, my dear, talk clearly, or we'll declare you
drunk and throw you out!

ALCIBIADES
My *angel*, your *slave* –

ANTAGORAS
Oh shut up, get on with it.

ALCIBIADES
Religion is knowledge, as Plato said. It's the knowledge of good
and evil. There!

PLATO
It's the *fight* between good and evil —

ALCIBIADES
Oh, no —

SOCRATES
What about power?

ALCIBIADES   *solemn and sonorous*
Knowledge is power, as we all know. Power is the *knowledge*
that good and evil are *not* enemies, they are *friends*. The human
soul is the seat of their harmony. The great chamber of the
perfect soul enshrines the secret love of good for evil and evil
for good. *That* union is what is absolute, and beautiful, and
real. We cannot overcome the darkness within, it's fundamental
and indestructible, we must cherish it, we must understand it
and love it. Good needs evil, it can only *exist* by contrast, wise
Heraclitus told us that, the struggle between the dark and the
light is a kind of life-giving play, a game played by lovers. So
evil isn't really evil, good isn't really good, we pass beyond the
ordinary childish abstract notions of good and evil, and enter
into the unity of the world! *Then* we are kings, *then* we are
gods, the unified soul is the lord of reality. *That's* religion,
that's the mystery which the initiated know, and *now is the
new era* when at last it will be made plain.

PLATO   *furious*
That's a damned lie, the worst lie of all, Good must *never* make
peace with evil, never, never! It must *kill* evil!

ALCIBIADES
You *are* bloodthirsty! Don't you want *harmony*, don't you

want to make something *creative* out of all that warfare that's going on inside you? Why be always tearing yourself to pieces? Don't you want human life to *work*, to *function*?

PLATO *incoherent*
That's perfect *muck*! Good must be pure and separate and – absolute – and – only what's completely good can – save us –

ALCIBIADES
But your perfectly pure good thing does not exist, that's the trouble, dear, all the world proves *that*!

PLATO
It *does*, it *must* – it's *more real* – I can't explain –

ALCIBIADES
My dear little one, I can see that you can't!

Plato hurls himself at Alcibiades. They fight. Alcibiades is stronger, twists Plato's arm.

ΑΓΑΘΟΣ
Don't hurt him!

ANTAGORAS *amused*
Sexual jealousy, I'm afraid!

Socrates is amused for a moment, then annoyed.

SOCRATES
Stop it, *stop it*!

He interferes, they separate. Socrates slaps Plato.

ALCIBIADES *laughing*
Creative strife! Homage to Heraclitus!

PLATO
I hate your ideas, I'd like to kill them!

SOCRATES
You can't kill ideas, you must learn to *think*.

ALCIBIADES
He will never think, he's a dreamy poet, that's what's so charming. What a fierce little kitten it is, pretty pussy!

SOCRATES
Don't torment him. [*To Plato*] I know you want to understand, perhaps you want to understand too much, you want to know too much. In philosophy we have to respect what we can't understand, just *look* at it and *describe* it.

ACASTOS
How do you mean?

SOCRATES
Stay close to what's obviously true, what people call common sense, what clever people may miss entirely. We've been told that religion is superstition, that it's socially useful, that it's the love of goodness, and now that it's the harmony of good and evil. But instead let's say something simple. The most important thing in life is virtue, and virtue isn't a mystery, it's truthfulness and justice and kindness and courage, things we understand. Anybody can *try* to be good, it's not obscure!

ACASTOS
But isn't religion the most important thing, if there is such a thing, *mustn't* it be?

SOCRATES
Beware in philosophy of things which 'must be so', at least look at them with a cool eye. Religion and virtue are not always allies, religion is many things and must be subject to justice and truth. We can't always learn virtue from loving good, we often have to live by external rules. But we are lovers and symbol-

makers and that is our talent for religion, which displays the absolute charm of virtue and how we can love it. Religious symbols are a natural, holy use of art. But of course, religion mustn't become magic. There's no secret knowledge, no complete explanation, we must be humble and simple and see what we know and respect what we don't know. Man is not the measure of all things, we don't just invent our values, we live by a higher law, yet we can't fully explain how this is so. [*To Plato*] Everything is in a way less deep and in a way deeper than you think. You want a long explanation, but in the end your explanation repeats what you knew at the start. You said yourself it was like remembering.

PLATO
But the unknown – isn't that the end of the way?

SOCRATES
There is no way, we are here now at the end, we have to do the nearest thing. We are not gods, we are absurd limited beings, we live with affliction and chance. The most important things are close to us, the truth is close, in front of our noses, like the faces of our friends, we need no expert to tell us. Religion is our love of virtue lightening the present moment. It is respect for what we know, and reverence for what we don't know, what we can only *approach*, where our not-knowing must be our mode of knowing, where we make symbols and images, and then destroy them, and make other ones, as we see now in our own time. Images are natural, art is natural, sacraments and pictures and holy things are natural, the inner and the outer reflect each other, there is a reverence which finds what is spiritual everywhere in the world, *he* is right [*pointing to the servant*], God is everywhere. If we love whatever God we know and speak to Him truthfully we shall be answered. Out at the very edge of our imagination the spirit is eternally active.

Respect the pure visions which speak to the heart, find there what is absolute. That is why we go to a holy place and kneel down. There is nothing more ultimate than that. [*Pause*]

PLATO
You, who know so much, tell us this!

SOCRATES
Because I do not know so much.

PLATO
But we *can* change, we *can* be enlightened, we *can* be saved?

SOCRATES
If we do good things which are near to us we may improve a little; don't make a drama of it, my dear. To tell the truth, that is an exercise which is always available. Goodness is simple, it's just very difficult.

Socrates is now smiling. He turns to Alcibiades.

ALCIBIADES
Oh you and your simplicity and your ignorance, how you drive us, you *herd* us into thinking!

SOCRATES
So – young Plato –

PLATO
I will kneel at this shrine.

SOCRATES
Well – by Zeus, if we want to see that torchlight procession we should go now! Let us enjoy our gods while we can. Come, Alcibiades. [*To Antagoras*] Thank you. [*To all*] Come, dear friends.

They rise for Socrates's departure. He goes, affectionately arm in arm with Alcibiades.

TIMONAX   *to Antagoras*
I want that boy!

Antagoras and Timonax depart arm in arm. Plato covers his face.

ACASTOS
You're jealous!

PLATO
It can't be so simple. Somehow I couldn't bear it to be simple! If only I could get it *clear*! [*He holds his bursting head.*]

ACASTOS
You never will. Anyway, let's be happy. Come, dear Plato.

Acastos puts his arm round Plato's waist, Plato resists, then accepts the gesture. Acastos pulls him away by the hand. The servant is left alone. He smiles, raising his arms as if in prayer.

The dialogues are designed to be performed either in modern dress or in period costume. In a period performance the servant in Above the Gods *will of course be a slave, and the following text may be preferred.*

TIMONAX
Well, if you want to go on and we want to rest why not question this black fellow? I know Socrates never needs a rest.

SOCRATES
What does Antagoras think? May we question the slave?

ANTAGORAS
Of course, Socrates, whatever you like.

SOCRATES
Does he speak Greek?

ANTAGORAS
Yes, he was bred on our country estate.

As they discuss the slave Acastos is uncomfortable, looks at Plato, who remains impassive.

TIMONAX
Has he got any religion?

ANTAGORAS
His mother was a Nubian, she probably had some superstitious belief. But he's a simple chap, he hasn't a single idea in his head, you see he isn't even listening, he's in another world.

TIMONAX
At least we can find out if religion is something natural!

SOCRATES
I would like Acastos to question the slave.

ACASTOS
Oh no! Please not!

SOCRATES
I won't always be here to ask questions, others must learn.
Besides you are young and gentle and won't upset him. Go on,
my dear.

ACASTOS *very nervous*
We are talking about religion. [*It takes a moment for him to
attract the slave's attention.*] Look – excuse me – we're –
talking about *religion.* You know what religion is?

*The slave is a graceful youth. He is a little timid at first but
soon shows no fear or embarrassment.*

SLAVE
No, sir.

TIMONAX
End of conversation.

SOCRATES
Go on, tell him what it is.

ACASTOS
Oh dear! I mean – when you go to the temples –

SLAVE
I never go to the temples, sir.

ACASTOS
Do you pray? Pray? say prayers?

SLAVE
I don't know, sir, I do not know what is that.

TIMONAX
Lucky fellow, no religion, that shows it isn't natural!

ACASTOS
Shall we stop here?

SOCRATES *observing the scene with some amusement*
No, go on.

ACASTOS
You know people believe in worship, and holy and sacred
things and places –

SLAVE
I don't know, sir.

TIMONAX
He's simple-minded.

ANTAGORAS
You're getting nowhere with religion, try morality.

ACASTOS *with a glance at Socrates*
Do you know what morality is, morals, duty –

SLAVE
No, sir.

SOCRATES
Explain it.

ACASTOS
Morality is – well [*Antagoras and Timonax giggle* .] Let me
see. When your conscience – no – when you feel something's
right, and you want to do it because it's right and good, and not
just because it's pleasant – For instance, when you make a
promise–[*Slave looks blank*] I mean–you do make promises–
sometimes, promise somebody something?

SLAVE
No. [*Explains*] I don't make, I don't know what is that thing.

ACASTOS *getting desperate*
But do you ever feel you *ought* to do something, that it's an *obligation*, when your heart tells you something *must* be done whether you like it or not?

SLAVE
No, sir, certainly not, sir.

ACASTOS
Why certainly not?

SLAVE *who thinks this is obvious*
I only do what I am told.

ACASTOS
I can't bear this!

ANTAGORAS
You see, they have no sense of duty, no idea of obligation, this is an important element in their condition, a merciful disability, like women, they simply lack the concept!

SOCRATES
Try to get back to religion.

ACASTOS
You know about rites and rituals, when people –

ANTAGORAS
He doesn't know these words.

ACASTOS
Like the procession this afternoon.

SLAVE *animated*
Oh yes, sir, the procession, that's good, when they dress up, so,

and there is such music, and the tambourines, bom bom, and the flowers, it is so beautiful, and my heart goes bom bom, and my feet go, go, go, oh yes, oh yes!

He takes a few steps. Timonax and Antagoras laugh, Socrates smiles. Acastos is touched and upset, Plato frowns slightly.

ANTAGORAS
I'm afraid this isn't getting us anywhere.

SOCRATES
Ask him about the gods.

TIMONAX
What's the use!

ACASTOS
Do you know what the gods are – have you heard of God or the gods?

SLAVE
Gods –

TIMONAX
Never heard of them.

SLAVE
Oh yes, sir, the gods, oh yes!

ACASTOS
Tell me about the gods, do you believe in them?

SLAVE
I don't understand, sir.

ACASTOS
So you don't believe in the gods, you think there are no gods?

SLAVE *amazed*
No gods?

ACASTOS
That's what you think?

SLAVE
How could I think that when I see them all the time?

ACASTOS
You *see* them? You mean their statues?

SLAVE
No, no, not statues, the *gods*, they are everywhere, you cannot help seeing them!

ANTAGORAS
Well, well!

ACASTOS
Where do you see them?

ANTAGORAS
Are they here?

SLAVE
No, sir, but they are in the garden and in the vineyard and in the trees and beside the river, oh so many gods!

ACASTOS *fascinated*
What are they like?

SLAVE
They are beautiful, oh so beautiful, the most beautiful of all!

ACASTOS
Are they good?

SLAVE *puzzled*
I don't know. They are gods.

ACASTOS
Do you talk to them?

SLAVE
Oh yes, I talk to them, much, much talk.

ACASTOS
And do they answer?

SLAVE
Well, sir, sometimes they laugh, they are often laughing, oh they are so happy!

ACASTOS
Do you pray to them? I mean do you ask them to give you things?

SLAVE
No, sir. What could they give me better than just to be there with me?

TIMONAX
Don't you ask them to make you free one day and not a slave?

SLAVE   *suddenly upset*
I don't know – that –

ACASTOS   *to Socrates*
Can we let him go?

Socrates nods, Antagoras makes a dismissive gesture, the slave departs. Acastos looks accusingly at Timonax.

ACASTOS
You shouldn't have said that!

TIMONAX   *ruefully*
All right! Let's just hope he hasn't got that concept either! But of course he was just putting on an act.

ANTAGORAS
No, no, there you have the childish superstitions of primitive people, they're like children.

ACASTOS

I don't think it's superstition.

TIMONAX

You think there really are gods and he really sees them? You should have asked him how large they are!

SOCRATES

Acastos means that for him there are gods. He is fortunate, he has happy gods. Thales tells us there are gods everywhere.

ANTAGORAS

That's poetic, just a metaphor.

SOCRATES

There are deep metaphors, perhaps there are bottomless metaphors.

At this point Socrates withdraws a little from the others and stands motionless in thought. They are used to this habit of his and lower their voices respectfully. They glance at him occasionally, put fingers to lips. Plato, watching Socrates intently, ignores their conversation.

ANTAGORAS

That slave, he's not much of a worker, he's too dreamy, we've put him on the list for the silver mines, they pay a lot for a healthy one.

TIMONAX

You're going to send that beautiful animal to the silver mines?

ACASTOS

You care because he's beautiful. You ought to care because he's human. They die like flies in the mines.

ANTAGORAS

There are things one doesn't talk about in polite society. There's nothing we can do, moaning about it is just sentimental hypocrisy. Without slavery our economy would collapse.

ACASTOS

I think slavery is retarding our economy. Anyway it's immoral.

TIMONAX

I don't like slavery but we've got to have it, it's a fact of life, always was, always will be.

ACASTOS

Slavery is contrary to nature.

ANTAGORAS

Slavery is a matter of fate.

ACASTOS

That's superstition!

ANTAGORAS

Slavery is a man's fate. It could be yours, it could be mine, where he is we might be. It's a humbling thought.

ACASTOS

But as it happens we're not where he is, and —

ANTAGORAS

There are those upon whom no light falls, it cannot be otherwise.

TIMONAX

Would you sell me that slave?

ANTAGORAS

What do you want him for?